RICE UNIVERSITY

SEMICENTENNIAL PUBLICATIONS

The Idea
of the South

EDITOR

FRANK E. VANDIVER

CONTRIBUTORS

RICHARD B. HARWELL

HUGH B. PATTERSON, JR.

LOUIS D. RUBIN, JR.

GEORGE B. TINDALL

FRANK E. VANDIVER

WALTER PRESCOTT WEBB

T. HARRY WILLIAMS

The Idea
of the South

PURSUIT OF A CENTRAL THEME

PUBLISHED FOR

WILLIAM MARSH RICE UNIVERSITY

BY

THE UNIVERSITY OF CHICAGO PRESS

Library of Congress Catalog Card Number: 64-15818

THE UNIVERSITY OF CHICAGO PRESS, CHICAGO & LONDON
The University of Toronto Press, Toronto 5, Canada

917.5
V245i

W_{HAT} is the South? Is there one? Or is the southern section of the United States more myth than substance? Some students have called the American West a "state of mind" and denied it as a true region. Does the South deserve similar short writ?

These questions beguile scholars, North and South, and have long fascinated novelists. It seemed highly appropriate that part of Rice University's fiftieth-anniversary observance should focus on the battle for the South—a battle which waxes unabated. Hence the History Department symposium on "The Idea of the South," which resulted in this volume.

Historians enter the battle for the South with myriad attempts to find a "central theme" in the section's past, a theme which will somehow articulate the ineffable. Novelists attack the South on multiple fronts; some frosting it in moonlight, magnolias, and plantations; others etching it in cruel lines of racist decadence; still others riming it in mystery. Generations of Southern writers have conceded the differentness of the South, conceded that a mystic world unlike the rest of America shimmers below Mason and Dixon's line. Even those who found it not the best of all possible worlds nonetheless confessed it different. But few have been satisfied with the available explanations of this difference; so each succeeding generation offers its own explanation and the issue grows geometrically confused.

Difference has never bothered Southerners; many, indeed, are proud of it, prefer it to sharing Yankee commonality. Over the course of the past century, in fact, Southern difference has been used effectively by the section in rebuffing modern times. Tradition has served as a guide for strong social conservatism, clanship has served as a bulwark against the state. And a surfeit of Negroes, legacies from slavery and the Civil War, imposed special burdens on the South which could hardly be conceived by the North, much less understood. Hence the plaint long echoed: "You don't understand our problem. You don't have great numbers of blacks to handle. Leave us alone to solve the problem our way." Difference in this case served as a convenient cloak for wrong. It became a staunch defense for the white supremacy which historian Ulrich B. Phillips saw as his "Central Theme of Southern History."

The presence of many Negroes, a special climate, a lengthy growing season, a dedication to old things—all these are conditions of the South. None really penetrates the South, illuminates its specialty, exposes its essence. Southern folk "talk funny" to people from other parts of the country, but their drawl marks them as Southerners. They cherish, many of them, vestiges of ancestor worship and are consequently self-revealed. It's easy to tell a Southerner. Can that be said of any Yankees, save, perhaps, Vermonters? Of Westerners? Of Los Angeleans? Perhaps the fact of recognition is evidence of identity.

But there must be more to it. Surely there lurks somewhere a South, a tangible, knowable, living South, with traditions and meanings and ideals to serve the present and future as well as the past. This unseen South must embrace all the Souths already mentioned, must stand testimony to easy life on plantations, to happy pickaninnies thronging "massa" as he walks the quarters, to long, gaunt lines of men in gray marching dusty roads into history, to the Henry Gradys with visions of industry and plenty, to the Ben Tillmans and Tom Watsons and Huey Longs with their perception of the little people, to the Joe Christmases, the Ab Snopeses and the human woe their lives transfigured, to the Martin Luther Kings and James Merediths and their revolution. The South must be all these things, these places; it must also be self-defining, self-contained, self-reliant, a section more than a section, a province, or a realm.

It may be that "What is it?" is the wrong, even the impossible, question. It may be that the South exists now, and has existed, as a place holding the virtues of the past against the buffets of change, the batters of the present, the agonies of the future. Possibly the South can be glimpsed only in passing, caught in fleeting image as time goes by. It may be that the South is something like Hesperides or Camelot, a place of good promise. If this be so, the South lingers on as a touchstone of the past, a bridge to the future. Surely this is no thin reality.

Be it what it may, the South was the subject of this symposium held at Rice University. To pursue and, hopefully, to elucidate the South, the History Department invited distinguished scholars of varied disciplines to participate in the symposium and to present papers on "The Idea of the South." Happily, though each worked independently, their labors produced a unified program, one which began with abstractions and moved toward reality, which encompassed both the South's nostalgia and its striving. A striking constant ran through all the discussions: the South is always changing. Is change, after all, the elusive Central Theme?

FRANK E. VANDIVER

Contents

GEORGE B. TINDALL

Mythology: A New Frontier in Southern History

THE IDEA of the South—or more appropriately, the ideas of the South—belong in large part to the order of social myth. There are few areas of the modern world that have bred a regional mythology so potent, so profuse and diverse, even so paradoxical, as the American South. But the various mythical images of the South that have so significantly affected American history have yet to be subjected to the kind of broad and imaginative historical analysis that has been applied to the idea of the American West, particularly in Henry Nash Smith's *Virgin Land: The American West as Symbol and Myth*. The idea of the South has yet to be fully examined in the context of mythology, as essentially a problem of intellectual history.

To place the ideas of the South in the context of mythology, of course, is not necessarily to pass judgment upon them as illusions. The game of debunking myths, Harry Levin has warned us, starts "in the denunciation of myth as falsehood from the vantage-point of a rival myth."[1] Mythology has other meanings, not all of them pejorative, and myths have a life of their own which to some degree renders irrelevant the question of their correlation to empirical fact. Setting aside for the moment the multiple connotations of the term, we may say that social myths in general, including those of the South, are simply mental pictures that portray the pattern of what a people think they are (or ought to be) or what somebody else thinks they are. They tend to develop

GEORGE B. TINDALL, Associate Professor of History, University of North Carolina, has been interested chiefly in the post-Reconstruction history of the South. Author of *South Carolina Negroes, 1877–1900* and numerous articles, Professor Tindall has been commissioned to write the final volume in the ten-volume "History of the South" series, sponsored jointly by Louisiana State University and the University of Texas.

[1] Harry Levin, "Some Meanings of Myth," in Henry A. Murray (ed.), *Myth and Mythmakers* (New York, 1960), p. 106.

abstract ideas in more or less concrete and dramatic terms. In the words of Henry Nash Smith, they fuse "concept and emotion into an image."[2]

They may serve a variety of functions. "A myth," Mark Schorer has observed, "is a large, controlling image that gives philosophical meaning to the facts of ordinary life; that is, which has organizing value for experience."[3] It may offer useful generalizations by which data may be tested. But being also "charged with values, aspirations, ideals and meanings,"[4] myths may become the ground for belief, for either loyalty and defense on the one hand or hostility and opposition on the other. In such circumstances a myth itself becomes one of the realities of history, significantly influencing the course of human action, for good or ill. There is, of course, always a danger of illusion, a danger that in ordering one's vision of reality, the myth may predetermine the categories of perception, rendering one blind to things that do not fit into the mental image.

Since the Southern mind is reputed to be peculiarly resistant to pure abstraction and more receptive to the concrete and dramatic image, it may be unusually susceptible to mythology. Perhaps for the same reason our subject can best be approached through reference to the contrasting experiences of two Southerners—one recent, the other about forty-five years ago.

The first is the experience of a contemporary Louisiana writer, John T. Westbrook.

During the thirties and early forties [Westbrook has written] when I was an English instructor at the University of Missouri, I was often mildly irritated by the average northerner's Jeeter-Lester-and-potlikker idea of the South. Even today the northern visitor inertia-headedly maintains his misconception: he hankers to see eroded hills and rednecks, scrub cotton and sharecropper shacks.

It little profits me to drive him through Baton Rouge, show him the oil-ethyl-rubber-aluminum-chemical miles of industry along the Mississippi River, and say, "This . . . is the fastest-growing city of over 100,000 in America. We can amply substantiate our claim that we are atomic target number one, that in the next war the Russians will obliterate us first. . . ."

Our northerner is suspicious of all this crass evidence presented to his senses. It bewilders and befuddles him. He is too deeply steeped in William Faulkner and Robert Penn Warren. The fumes of progress are in his nose and the bright steel of industry towers before his eyes, but his heart is away in Yoknapataw-

[2] Henry Nash Smith, *Virgin Land: The American West as Symbol and Myth* (Vintage ed., New York, 1957), p. v.

[3] Mark Schorer, "The Necessity for Myth," in Murray (ed.), *Myth and Mythmakers*, p. 355.

[4] C. Vann Woodward, "The Antislavery Myth," *American Scholar*, XXXI (Spring, 1962), 325.

pha County with razorback hogs and night riders. On this trip to the South he wants, above all else, to sniff the effluvium of backwoods-and-sand-hill sub-humanity and to see at least one barn burn at midnight. So he looks at me with crafty misgiving, as if to say, "Well, you *do* drive a Cadillac, talk rather glibly about Kierkegaard and Sartre . . . but, after all, you *are* only fooling, aren't you? You do, don't you, sometimes, go out secretly by owl-light to drink swamp water and feed on sowbelly and collard greens?"[5]

The other story was the experience of a Southern historian, Frank L. Owsley, who traveled during World War I from Chicago via Cincinnati to Montgomery with a group of young ladies on the way to visit their menfolk at an army camp. He wrote later that, "despite everything which had ever been said to the contrary," the young ladies had a ro-mantic conception of the "Sunny South" and looked forward to the journey with considerable excitement. "They expected to enter a pleas-ant land of white columned mansions, green pastures, expansive cotton and tobacco fields where negroes sang spirituals all the day through." Except in the bluegrass basins of central Kentucky and Tennessee, what they actually found "were gutted hill-sides; scrub oak and pine; bramble and blackberry thickets, bottom lands once fertile now senile and ex-hausted, with spindling tobacco, corn, or cotton stalks . . . ; unpainted houses which were hardly more than shacks or here and there the crumbling ruins of old mansions covered with briars, the homes of snakes and lizards."[6] The disappointment of Dr. Owsley's ladies was, no doubt, even greater than that of Mr. Westbrook's friend in Baton Rouge.

There is a striking contrast between these two episodes, both in the picture of Southern reality and in the differing popular images that they present. The fact that they are four decades apart helps to account for the discrepancies, but what is not apparent at first is the common ances-try of the two images. They are not very distant cousins, collateral descendants from the standard image of the Old South, the plantation myth. The version of Owsley's lady friends is closer to the original primogenitor, which despite its advancing age and debility, still lives amid a flourishing progeny of legendary Southern gentility. According to Francis Pendleton Gaines, author of *The Southern Plantation*, the pat-tern appeared full-blown at least as early as 1832 in John Pendleton Kennedy's romance, *Swallow Barn*.[7] It has had a long career in story

[5] John T. Westbrook, "Twilight of Southern Regionalism," *Southwest Review*, XLII (Summer, 1957), 231.

[6] Frank L. Owsley, "The Old South and the New," *American Review*, VI (February, 1936), 475.

[7] Francis Pendleton Gaines, *The Southern Plantation: A Study in the Development and Accuracy of a Tradition* (New York, 1925), p. 23.

and novel and song, in the drama and motion picture. The corrosions of age seem to have ended its Hollywood career, although the old films still turn up on the late late. It may still be found in the tourist bait of shapely beauties in hoop skirts posed against the backdrop of white columns at Natchez, Orton, or a hundred other places.

These pictures are enough to trigger in the mind the whole euphoric pattern of kindly old marster with his mint julep; happy darkies singing in fields perpetually white to the harvest or, as the case may be, sadly recalling the long lost days of old; coquettish belles wooed by slender gallants in gray underneath the moonlight and magnolias. It is a pattern that yields all too easily to caricature and ridicule, for in its more sophisticated versions the figure of the planter carries a heavy freight of the aristocratic virtues: courtliness, grace, hospitality, honor, *noblesse oblige*, as well as many no less charming aristocratic vices: a lordly indifference to the balance sheet, hot temper, profanity, overindulgence, a certain stubborn obstinacy. The old-time Negro, when not a figure of comedy, is the very embodiment of loyalty. And the Southern belle: "Beautiful, graceful, accomplished in social charm, bewitching in coquetry, yet strangely steadfast in soul," Gaines has written, "she is perhaps the most winsome figure in the whole field of our fancy."[8] "The plantation romance," Gaines says, "remains our chief social idyl of the past; of an Arcadian scheme of existence, less material, less hurried, less prosaically equalitarian, less futile, richer in picturesqueness, festivity, in realized pleasure that recked not of hope or fear or unrejoicing labor."[9]

But there is still more to the traditional pattern. Somewhere off in the piney woods and erosion-gutted clay hills, away from the white columns and gentility, there existed Po' White Trash: the crackers; hillbillies; sand-hillers; rag, tag, and bobtail; squatters; "po' buckra" to the Negroes; the Ransy Sniffle of A. B. Longstreet's *Georgia Scenes* and his literary descendants like Jeeter Lester and Ab Snopes, abandoned to poverty and degeneracy—the victims, it was later discovered, of hookworm, malaria, and pellagra. Somewhere in the pattern the respectable small farmer was lost from sight. He seemed to be neither romantic nor outrageous enough to fit in. His neglect provides the classic example in Southern history of the blind spots engendered by the power of mythology. It was not until the 1930's that Frank L. Owsley and his students at Vanderbilt rediscovered the Southern yeoman farmer as the characteristic, or at least the most numerous, ante bellum white Southerner.[10] More about the yeoman presently; neglected in the plantation myth, he was in the foreground of another.

[8] *Ibid.*, p. 16.   [9] *Ibid.*, p. 4.

[10] Frank L. Owsley, *Plain Folk of the Old South* (Baton Rouge, 1949).

In contrast to the legitimate heirs of the plantation myth, the image of John T. Westbrook's Yankee visitor in Baton Rouge seems to be descended from what might be called the illegitimate line of the plantation myth, out of abolition. It is one of the ironies of our history that, as Gaines put it, the "two opposing sides of the fiercest controversy that ever shook national thought agreed concerning certain picturesque elements of plantation life and joined hands to set the conception unforgettably in public consciousness."[11] The abolitionists found it difficult, or even undesirable, to escape the standard image. It was pretty fully developed even in *Uncle Tom's Cabin.* Harriet Beecher Stowe made her villain a Yankee overseer, and has been accused by at least one latter-day abolitionist of implanting deeply in the American mind the stereotype of the faithful darkey. For others the plantation myth simply appeared in reverse, as a pattern of corrupt opulence resting upon human exploitation. Gentle old marster became the arrogant, haughty, imperious potentate, the very embodiment of sin, the central target of the antislavery attack. He maintained a seraglio in the slave quarters; he bred Negroes like cattle and sold them down the river to certain death in the sugar mills, separating families if that served his purpose, while Southern women suffered in silence the guilty knowledge of their men's infidelity. The happy darkies in this picture became white men in black skins, an oppressed people longing for freedom, the victims of countless atrocities so ghastly as to be unbelievable except for undeniable evidence, forever seeking an opportunity to follow the North Star to freedom. The masses of the white folks were simply poor whites, relegated to ignorance and degeneracy by the slavocracy.

Both lines of the plantation myth have been remarkably prolific, but the more adaptable one has been that of the abolitionists. It has repeatedly readjusted to new conditions while the more legitimate line has courted extinction, running out finally into the decadence perpetrated by Tennessee Williams. Meanwhile, the abolitionist image of brutality persisted through and beyond Reconstruction in the Republican outrage mills and bloody shirt political campaigns. For several decades it was more than overbalanced by the Southern image of Reconstruction horrors, disarmed by prophets of a New South created in the image of the North, and almost completely submerged under the popularity of plantation romances in the generation before Owsley's trainload of ladies ventured into their "Sunny South" of the teens. At about that time, however, the undercurrents began to emerge once again into the mainstream of American thought. In the clever decade of the twenties a kind of neo-abolitionist myth of the Savage South was compounded. It seemed that the benighted South, after a period of relative neglect, suddenly became

[11] Gaines, *The Southern Plantation,* p. 30.

an object of concern to every publicist in the country. One Southern abomination after another was ground through their mills: child labor, peonage, lynching, hookworm, pellagra, the Scopes trial, the Fundamentalist crusade against Al Smith. The guiding genius was Henry L. Mencken, the hatchet man from Baltimore who developed the game of South-baiting into a national pastime, a fine art at which he had no peer. In 1917, when he started constructing his image of "Baptist and Methodist barbarism" below the Potomac, he began with the sterility of Southern literature and went on from there. With characteristic glee he anointed one J. Gordon Coogler of South Carolina "the last bard of Dixie" and quoted his immortal couplet:

> Alas, for the South! Her books have grown fewer—
> She never was much given to literature.

"Down there," Mencken wrote, "a poet is now almost as rare as an oboe-player, a dry-point etcher or a metaphysician." As for "critics, musical composers, painters, sculptors, architects . . . there is not even a bad one between the Potomac mud-flats and the Gulf. Nor an historian. Nor a sociologist. Nor a philosopher. Nor a theologian. Nor a scientist. In all these fields the south is an awe-inspiring blank. . . ."[12] It was as complete a vacuity as the interstellar spaces, the "Sahara of the Bozart," "The Bible Belt." He summed it all up in one basic catalogue of Southern grotesqueries: "Fundamentalism, Ku Kluxry, revivals, lynchings, hog wallow politics—these are the things that always occur to a northerner when he thinks of the south."[13] The South, in short, had fallen prey to its poor whites, who would soon achieve apotheosis in the Snopes family.

It did not end with the twenties. The image was reinforced by a variety of episodes: the Scottsboro trials, chain gang exposés, Bilbo and Rankin, Senate filibusters, labor wars; much later by Central High and Orval Faubus, Emmett Till and Autherine Lucy and James Meredith, bus boycotts and Freedom Riders; and not least of all by the lush growth of literature that covered Mencken's Sahara, with Caldwell's *Tobacco Road* and Faulkner's *Sanctuary* and various other products of what Ellen Glasgow labeled the Southern Gothic and a less elegant Mississippi editor called the "privy school" of literature. In the words of Faulkner's character, Gavin Stevens, the North suffered from a curious "gullibility: a volitionless, almost helpless capacity and eagerness to believe

---

[12] Henry L. Mencken, "The Sahara of the Bozart," in *Prejudices: Second Series* (New York, 1920), pp. 136, 137, 139.

[13] Henry L. Mencken, "The South Rebels Again," in Robert McHugh (ed.), *The Bathtub Hoax and Other Blasts & Bravos from the Chicago Tribune* (New York, 1958), p. 249. From a column in the Chicago *Tribune*, December 7, 1924.

anything about the South not even provided it be derogatory but merely bizarre enough and strange enough."[14] And Faulkner, to be sure, did not altogether neglect that market. Not surprisingly, he was taken in some quarters for a realist, and the image of Southern savagery long obscured the critics' recognition of his manifold merits.

The family line of the plantation myth can be traced only so far in the legendary gentility and savagery of the South. Other family lines seem to be entirely independent—if sometimes on friendly terms. In an excellent study, "The New South Creed, 1865–1900," soon to be published, Paul M. Gaston has traced the evolution of the creed into a genuine myth. In the aftermath of the Civil War, apostles of a "New South," led by Henry W. Grady, preached with almost evangelical fervor the gospel of industry. Their dream, Gaston writes, "was essentially a promise of American life for the South. It proffered all the glitter and glory and freedom from guilt that inhered in the American ideal."[15] From advocacy, from this vision of the future, the prophets soon advanced to the belief that "their promised land [was] at hand, no longer merely a gleaming goal." "By the twentieth century . . . there was established for many in the South a pattern of belief within which they could see themselves and their section as rich, success-oriented, and just . . . opulence and power were at hand . . . the Negro lived in the best of all possible worlds."[16]

As the twentieth century advanced, and wealth did in fact increase, the creed of the New South took on an additional burden of crusades for good roads and education, blending them into what Francis B. Simkins has called the "trinity of Southern progress": industrial growth, good roads, and schools. When the American Historical Association went to Durham in 1929 for its annual meeting, Robert D. W. Connor of the University of North Carolina presented the picture of a rehabilitated South that had "shaken itself free from its heritage of war and Reconstruction. Its self-confidence restored, its political stability assured, its prosperity regained, its social problems on the way to solution. . . ."[17] Two months before Connor spoke, the New York Stock Exchange had broken badly, and in the aftermath the image he described was seriously blurred, but before the end of the thirties it was being brought back into focus by renewed industrial expansion that received increased momentum from World War II and postwar prosperity.

[14] William Faulkner, *Intruder in the Dust* (New York, 1948), p. 153.

[15] Paul Morton Gaston, "The New South Creed, 1865–1900" (Ph.D. dissertation, Department of History, University of North Carolina, 1961), p. 193.

[16] *Ibid.*, pp. 195, 216.

[17] Robert D. W. Connor, "The Rehabilitation of a Rural Commonwealth," *American Historical Review*, XXXVI (October, 1930), 62.

Two new and disparate images emerged in the depression years, both with the altogether novel feature of academic trappings and affiliations. One was the burgeoning school of sociological regionalism led by Howard W. Odum and Rupert B. Vance at the University of North Carolina. It was neither altogether the image of the Savage South nor that of industrial progress, although both entered into the compound. It was rather a concept of the "Problem South," which Franklin D. Roosevelt labeled "the Nation's Economic Problem No. 1," a region with indisputable shortcomings but with potentialities that needed constructive attention and the application of rational social planning. Through the disciples of Odum as well as the agencies of the New Deal, the vision issued in a flood of social science monographs and programs for reform and development. To one undergraduate in Chapel Hill at the time, it seemed in retrospect that "we had more of an attitude of service to the South as the South than was true later. . . ."[18]

The regionalists were challenged by the Vanderbilt Agrarians, who developed a myth of the traditional South. Their manifesto, *I'll Take My Stand*, by Twelve Southerners, appeared by fortuitous circumstance in 1930 when industrial capitalism seemed on the verge of collapse. In reaction against both the progressive New South and Mencken's image of savagery they championed, in Donald Davidson's words, a "traditional society . . . that is stable, religious, more rural than urban, and politically conservative," in which human needs were supplied by "Family, bloodkinship, clanship, folkways, custom, community. . . ."[19] The ideal of the traditional virtues took on the texture of myth in their image of the agrarian South. Of course, in the end, their agrarianism proved less important as a social-economic force than as a context for creative literature. The central figures in the movement were the Fugitive poets John Crowe Ransom, Donald Davidson, Allen Tate, and Robert Penn Warren. But, as Professor Louis Rubin has emphasized, "Through their vision of an agrarian community, the authors of *I'll Take My Stand* presented a critique of the modern world. In contrast to the hurried, nervous life of cities, the image of the agrarian South was of a life in which human beings existed serenely and harmoniously." Their critique of the modern frenzy "has since been echoed by commentator after commentator."[20]

[18] Alexander Heard, quoted in Wilma Dykeman and James Stokely, *Seeds of Southern Change: The Life of Will Alexander* (Chicago, 1962), p. 303.

[19] Donald Davidson, "Why the Modern South Has a Great Literature," *Vanderbilt Studies in the Humanities*, I (1951), 12.

[20] Louis D. Rubin, Jr., "Introduction to the Torchbook Edition," in Twelve Southerners, *I'll Take My Stand* (Torchbook ed.; New York, 1962), pp. xiv, xvii. See also Herman Clarence Nixon, "A Thirty Years' Personal View," *Mississippi Quarterly*, XIII (Spring, 1960), 79, for parallels in recent social criticism.

While it never became altogether clear whether the Agrarians were celebrating the aristocratic graces or following the old Jeffersonian dictum that "Those who labor in the earth are the chosen people of God . . . ," most of them seemed to come down eventually on the side of the farmer rather than the planter. Frank L. Owsley, who rediscovered the ante bellum yeoman farmer, was one of them. Insofar as they extolled the yeoman farmer, the Agrarians laid hold upon an image older than any of the others—the Jeffersonian South. David M. Potter, a Southerner in exile at Stanford University, has remarked how difficult it is for many people to realize that the benighted South "was, until recently, regarded by many liberals as the birthplace and the natural bulwark of the Jeffersonian ideal. . . ."[21] The theme has long had an appeal for historians as well as others. Frederick Jackson Turner developed it for the West and William E. Dodd for the South. According to Dodd the democratic, equalitarian South of the Jeffersonian image was the norm; the plantation slavocracy was the great aberration. Dodd's theme has been reflected in the writing of other historians, largely in terms of a region subjected to economic colonialism by an imperial Northeast: Charles A. Beard, for example, who saw the sectional conflict as a struggle between agrarianism and industrialism; Howard K. Beale, who interpreted Reconstruction in similar terms; C. Vann Woodward, defender of Populism; Arthur S. Link, who first rediscovered the Southern progressives; and Walter Prescott Webb, who found the nation divided between an exploited South and West on the one hand, and a predatory Northeast on the other. Jefferson, like the South, it sometimes seems, can mean all things to all men, and the Jefferson image of agrarian democracy has been a favorite recourse of Southern liberals, just as his state-rights doctrines have nourished conservatism.

In stark contrast to radical agrarianism there stands the concept of monolithic conservatism in Southern politics. It seems to be a proposition generally taken for granted now that the South is, by definition, conservative—and always has been. Yet the South in the late nineteenth century produced some of the most radical Populists and in the twentieth was a bulwark of Wilsonian progressivism and Roosevelt's New Deal, at least up to a point. A good case has been made out by Arthur S. Link that Southern agrarian radicals pushed Wilson further into progressivism than he intended to go.[22] During the twenties Southern minority leadership in Congress kept up such a running battle against the conservative tax policies of Andrew Mellon that, believe it or not, there was real fear among some Northern businessmen during the 1932 cam-

---

[21] David M. Potter, "The Enigma of the South," *Yale Review*, LI (Autumn, 1961), 143.

[22] Arthur S. Link, "The South and the 'New Freedom': An Interpretation," *American Scholar*, XX (Summer, 1951), 314–24.

paign that Franklin D. Roosevelt might be succeeded by that radical Southern income-taxer, John Nance Garner![23] The conservative image of course has considerable validity, but it obscures understanding of such phenomena as Albert Gore, Russell Long, Lister Hill, John Sparkman, Olin D. Johnston, William Fulbright, the Yarboroughs of Texas, or the late Estes Kefauver. In the 1960 campaign the conservative image seriously victimized Lyndon B. Johnson, who started in politics as a vigorous New Dealer and later maneuvered through the Senate the first civil rights legislation since Reconstruction.

The infinite variety of Southern mythology could be catalogued and analyzed endlessly. A suggestive list would include the Proslavery South; the Confederate South; the Demagogic South; the State Rights South; the Fighting South; the Lazy South; the Folklore South; the South of jazz and the blues; the Booster South; the Rapacious South running away with Northern industries; the Liberal South of the interracial movement; the White Supremacy South of racial segregation, which seems to be for some the all-encompassing "Southern way of life"; the Anglo-Saxon (or was it the Scotch-Irish?) South, the most American of all regions because of its native population; or the Internationalist South, a mainstay of the Wilson, Roosevelt, and Truman foreign policies.

The South, then, has been the seedbed for a proliferation of paradoxical myths, all of which have some basis in empirical fact and all of which doubtlessly have, or have had, their true believers. The result has been, in David Potter's words, that the South has become an enigma, "a kind of Sphinx on the American land."[24] What is really the answer to the riddle, what is at bottom the foundation of Southern distinctiveness has never been established with finality, but the quest for a central theme of Southern history has repeatedly engaged the region's historians. Like Frederick Jackson Turner, who extracted the essential West in his frontier thesis, Southern historians have sought to distill the quintessence of the South into some kind of central theme.

In a recent survey of these efforts David L. Smiley of Wake Forest College has concluded that they turn upon two basic lines of thought: "the causal effects of environment, and the development of certain acquired characteristics of the people called Southern."[25] The distinctive climate and weather of the South, it has been argued, slowed the pace of life, tempered the speech of the South, dictated the system of staple

[23] A. G. Hopkins to Sam Rayburn, July 29, 1932; Rayburn to J. Andrew West, October 26, 1932, in Sam Rayburn Library, Bonham, Texas.

[24] Potter, "The Enigma of the South," p. 142.

[25] David L. Smiley, "The Quest for the Central Theme in Southern History," paper read before the Southern Historical Association, Miami Beach, Florida, November 8, 1962, p. 2.

crops and Negro slavery—in short, predetermined the plantation economy. The more persuasive suggestions have resulted from concentration
upon human factors and causation. The best known is that set forth by
U. B. Phillips. The quintessence of Southernism, he wrote in 1928, was
"a common resolve indomitably maintained" that the South "shall be
and remain a white man's country." Whether "expressed with the
frenzy of a demagogue or maintained with a patrician's quietude," this
was "the cardinal test of a Southerner and the central theme of Southern
history."[26] Other historians have pointed to the rural nature of Southern
society as the basic conditioning factor, to the prevalence of the country
gentleman ideal imported from England, to the experience of the South
as a conscious minority unified by criticism and attack from outside, to
the fundamental piety of the Bible Belt, and to various other factors. It
has even been suggested by one writer that a chart of the mule population would determine the boundaries of the South.

More recently, two historians have attempted new explanations. In
his search for a Southern identity, C. Vann Woodward advances several
crucial factors: the experience of poverty in a land of plenty; failure and
defeat in a land that glorifies success; sin and guilt amid the legend of
American innocence; and a sense of place and belonging among a people
given to abstraction.[27] David M. Potter, probing the enigma of the
South, has found the key to the riddle in the prevalence of a folk society. "This folk culture, we know, was far from being ideal or utopian," he writes, "and was in fact full of inequality and wrong, but if
the nostalgia persists was it because even the inequality and wrong were
parts of a life that still had a relatedness and meaning which our more
bountiful life in the mass culture seems to lack?"[28]

It is significant that both explanations are expressed largely in the
past tense, Potter's explicitly in terms of nostalgia. They recognize, by
implication at least, still another image—that of the Dynamic or the
Changing South. The image may be rather nebulous and the ultimate
ends unclear, but the fact of change is written inescapably across the
Southern scene. The consciousness of change has been present so long
as to become in itself one of the abiding facts of Southern life. Surely, it
was a part of the inspiration for the symposium that resulted in this
volume. As far back as the twenties it was the consciousness of change
that quickened the imaginations of a cultivated and sensitive minority,
giving us the Southern renaissance in literature. The peculiar historical

[26] Ulrich B. Phillips, "The Central Theme of Southern History," in E. Merton Coulter
(ed.), *The Course of the South to Secession* (New York, 1939), p. 152.

[27] C. Vann Woodward, "The Search for a Southern Identity," in *The Burden of Southern
History* (Baton Rouge, 1960), pp. 3–25.

[28] Potter, "The Enigma of the South," p. 151.

consciousness of the Southern writer, Allen Tate has suggested, "made possible the curious burst of intelligence that we get at a crossing of the ways, not unlike, on an infinitesmal scale, the outburst of poetic genius at the end of the sixteenth century when commercial England had already begun to crush feudal England."[29] Trace it through modern Southern writing, and at the center—in Ellen Glasgow, in Faulkner, Wolfe, Caldwell, the Fugitive-Agrarian poets, and all the others—there is the consciousness of change, of suspension between two worlds, a double focus looking both backward and forward.

The Southerner of the present generation has seen the old landmarks crumble with great rapidity: the one-crop agriculture and the very predominance of agriculture itself, the one-party system, the white primary, the poll tax, racial segregation, the poor white (at least in his classic connotations), the provincial isolation—virtually all the foundations of the established order. Yet, sometimes, the old traditions endure in surprising new forms. Southern folkways have been carried even into the factory, and the Bible Belt has revealed resources undreamed of in Mencken's philosophy—but who, in the twenties, could have anticipated Martin Luther King?

One wonders what new images, what new myths, might be nurtured by the emerging South. Some, like Harry Ashmore, have merely written *An Epitaph for Dixie*. It is the conclusion of two Southern sociologists, John M. Maclachlan and Joe S. Floyd, Jr., that present trends "might well hasten the day when the South, once perhaps the most distinctively 'different' American region, will have become . . . virtually indistinguishable from the other urban-industrial areas of the nation."[30] U. B. Phillips long ago suggested that the disappearance of race as a major issue would end Southern distinctiveness. One may wonder if Southern distinctiveness might even be preserved in new conditions entirely antithetic to his image. Charles L. Black, Jr., another *émigré* Southerner (at Yale Law School) has confessed to a fantastic dream that Southern whites and Negroes, bound in a special bond of common tragedy, may come to recognize their kinship. There is not the slightest warrant for it, he admits, in history, sociology, or common sense. But if it should come to pass, he suggests, "The South, which has always felt itself reserved for a high destiny, would have found it, and would have come to flower at last. And the fragrance of it would spread, beyond calculation, over the world."[31]

[29] Allen Tate, "The New Provincialism," *Virginia Quarterly Review*, XXI (Spring, 1945), 272.

[30] John M. Maclachlan and Joe S. Floyd, Jr., *This Changing South* (Gainesville, Fla., 1956), p. 151.

[31] Charles L. Black, Jr., "Paths to Desegregation," *New Republic*, CXXXVII (October 21, 1957), 15.

Despite the consciousness of change, perhaps even more because of it, Southerners still feel a persistent pull toward identification with their native region as a ground for belief and loyalty. Is there not yet something more than nostalgia to the idea of the South? Is there not some living heritage with which the modern Southerner can identify? Is there not, in short, a viable myth of the South? The quest for myth has been a powerful factor in recent Southern literature, and the suspicion is strong that it will irresistibly affect any historian's quest for the central theme of Southern history. It has all too clearly happened before—in the climatic theory, for example, which operated through its geographical determinism to justify the social order of the plantation, or the Phillips thesis of white supremacy, which has become almost a touchstone of the historian's attitude toward the whole contemporary issue of race. "To elaborate a central theme," David L. Smiley has asserted, is "but to reduce a multi-faceted story to a single aspect, and its result . . . but to find new footnotes to confirm revealed truths and prescribed views."[32] The trouble is that the quest for the central theme, like Turner's frontier thesis, becomes absorbed willy-nilly into the process of myth making.

To pursue the Turner analogy a little further, the conviction grows that the frontier thesis, with all its elaborations and critiques, has been exhausted (and in part exploded) as a source of new historical insight. It is no derogation of insights already gained to suggest that the same thing has happened to the quest for the central theme, and that the historian, *as historian*, may be better able to illuminate our understanding of the South now by turning to a new focus upon the regional mythology.

To undertake the analysis of mythology will no longer require him to venture into uncharted wilderness. A substantial conceptual framework of mythology has already been developed by anthropologists, philosophers, psychologists, theologians, and literary critics. The historian, while his field has always been closely related to mythology, has come only lately to the critique of it. But there now exists a considerable body of historical literature on the American national mythology and the related subject of the national character, and Smith's stimulating *Virgin Land* suggests the trails that may be followed into the idea of the South.

Several trails, in fact, have already been blazed. Nearly forty years ago, Francis Pendleton Gaines successfully traced the rise and progress of the plantation myth, and two recent authors have belatedly taken to the same trail. Howard R. Floan has considerably increased our knowledge of the abolitionist version in his study of Northern writers, *The South in Northern Eyes*, while William R. Taylor has approached the

---

[32] Smiley, "The Quest for the Central Theme in Southern History," p. 1.

subject from an entirely new perspective in his *Cavalier and Yankee*. Shields McIlwaine has traced the literary image of the poor white, while Stanley Elkins' *Slavery* has broken sharply from established concepts on both sides of that controversial question.[33] One foray into the New South has been made in Paul Gaston's "The New South Creed, 1865–1900." Yet many important areas—the Confederate and Reconstruction myths, for example—still remain almost untouched.

Some of the basic questions that need to be answered have been attacked in these studies; some have not. It is significant that students of literature have led the way and have pointed up the value of even third-rate creative literature in the critique of myth. The historian, however, should be able to contribute other perspectives. With his peculiar time perspective he can seek to unravel the tangled genealogy of myth that runs back from the modern Changing South to Jefferson's yeoman and Kennedy's plantation. Along the way he should investigate the possibility that some obscure dialectic may be at work in the pairing of obverse images: the two versions of the plantation, New South and Old, Cavalier and Yankee, genteel and savage, regionalist and agrarian, nativist and internationalist.

What, the historian may ask, have been the historical origins and functions of the myths? The plantation myth, according to Gaines and Floan, was born in the controversy and emotion of the struggle over slavery. It had polemical uses for both sides. Taylor, on the other hand, finds it origin in the psychological need, both North and South, to find a corrective for the grasping, materialistic, rootless society symbolized by the image of the Yankee. Vann Woodward and Gaston have noted its later psychological uses in bolstering the morale of the New South. The image of the Savage South has obvious polemical uses, but has it not others? Has it not served the function of national catharsis? Has it not created for many Americans a convenient scapegoat upon which the sins of all may be symbolically laid and thereby expiated—a most convenient escape from problem solving?[34] To what extent, indeed, has the mythology of the South in general welled up from the subconscious depths? Taylor, especially, has emphasized this question, but the skeptical historian will also be concerned with the degree to which it has been the

[33] Howard R. Floan, *The South in Northern Eyes, 1831–1860* (Austin, 1958); William R. Taylor, *Cavalier and Yankee: The Old South and American National Character* (New York, 1961); Shields McIlwaine, *The Southern Poor White from Lubberland to Tobacco Road* (Norman, Okla., 1939); Stanley M. Elkins, *Slavery: A Problem in American Institutional and Intellectual Life* (Chicago, 1959).

[34] "In a sense, the southern writer has been a scapegoat for his fellow Americans, for in taking his guilt upon himself and dramatizing it he has borne the sins of us all." C. Hugh Holman, "The Southerner as American Writer," in Charles Grier Sellers, Jr. (ed.), *The Southerner as American* (Chapel Hill, 1960), p. 199.

product or the device of deliberate manipulation by propagandists and vested interests seeking identification with the "real" South.

Certainly any effort to delineate the unique character of a people must take into account its mythology. "Poets," James G. Randall suggested, "have done better in expressing this oneness of the South than historians in explaining it."[35] Can it be that the historians have been looking in the wrong places, that they have failed to seek the key to the enigma where the poets have so readily found it—in the mythology that has had so much to do with shaping character, unifying society, developing a sense of community, of common ideals and shared goals, making the region conscious of its distinctiveness?[36] Perhaps by turning to different and untrodden paths we shall encounter the central theme of Southern history at last on the new frontier of mythology.

[35] James G. Randall, *The Civil War and Reconstruction* (Boston, 1937), pp. 3–4.

[36] Josiah Royce's definition of a "province" is pertinent here: ". . . any one part of a national domain which is geographically and socially sufficiently unified to have a true consciousness of its own ideals and customs and to possess a sense of its distinction from other parts of the country." Quoted in Frederick Jackson Turner, *The Significance of Sections in American History* (New York, 1932), p. 45.

RICHARD B. HARWELL

The Stream of Self-Consciousness

THERE ARE many Souths. The South, like the rest of America, is an ever changing land, reflecting itself differently in the eyes of different beholders and changing even, from time to time and from one area to another, in the eyes of the same beholder.

There is the South of tradition, a pleasant never-never land in which much that never existed is remembered as the backbone of its culture. And there is the South of a real and honest tradition of a yeoman aristocracy with its own way of life. There is the South of the radio, television, or comic-strip stereotype. There is the equally stereotyped South of tobacco roads and streetcars named Desire. There is the South of the apologist historian—a breed now largely passing. Fortunately, there is also the South of such genuinely good historians as Vann Wood-ward and T. Harry Williams. There is the South as seen by outsiders; or there is the South as seen by Southerners. Politicians view it in one light, historians in another, novelists or sociologists or economists in yet others. And all these Souths are real.

I am a Southerner. I stand proud of much of the South's past, much of her present, much of her future. I remember a South of quiet, rural life in Georgia and Virginia, of life in an abundantly vigorous and ambitious city as I grew up in Atlanta. I know the stultification of living too much in the past, as in certain parts of Virginia, and the phoniness of imitating too much of the bad from other places, as in Miami. I am also ashamed of my region—ashamed that it has taken nearly a hundred years for the South to begin to recognize honestly that she could not call off the result of the Civil War, ashamed that she has withheld herself, as something apart, from the rest of the nation, ashamed that the stereotype derived from her politicians (who, by and large, are far behind the thinking of

RICHARD B. HARWELL, Librarian, Bowdoin College, is a distinguished student of Southern belles-lettres and an accomplished bibliographer. He recently condensed Douglas Freeman's four-volume *R. E. Lee* into the one-volume *Lee* and is now working on a similar abridgment of Freeman's seven-volume *George Washington*.

their constituents) is the face she most often presents to the rest of America. I am ashamed of a fight against the law of our land that has made "all deliberate speed" mean "no speed at all." I am proud of the talents of the South, but ashamed of the waste of brainpower as too much of these talents are directed at blocking the inevitable. I am ashamed of Mississippi, but proud that only in that one state is segregation still supported with such near unanimity.

I am a Southerner. I remember with an ineffable nostalgia the magnificent passage about my native Georgia that is a part of Stephen Vincent Benét's *John Brown's Body:*[1]

It is not lucky to dream such stuff—

. . . .

Riding back through the Georgia fall
To the white-pillared porch of Wingate Hall.
Fall of the possum, fall of the 'coon,
And the lop-eared hound-dog baying the moon.
Fall that is neither bitter nor swift
But a brown girl bearing an idle gift,
A brown seed-kernel that splits apart
And shows the summer yet in its heart,
A smokiness so vague in the air
You feel it rather than see it there,
A brief, white rime on the red clay road
And slow mules creaking a lazy load
Through endless acres of afternoon,
A pine-cone fire and a banjo-tune,
And a julep mixed with a silver spoon.
Your noons are hot, your nights deep starred,
There is honeysuckle still in the yard,
Fall of the quail and the firefly-glows
And the pot-pourri of the rambler rose,
Fall that brings no promise of snows.

. . . .

This was his Georgia, this his share
Of pine and river and sleepy air,
Of summer thunder and winter rain
That spills bright tears on the window-pane
With the slight, fierce passion of young men's grief,
Of the mocking-bird and the mulberry leaf,
For, wherever the winds of Georgia run,
It smells of peaches long in the sun,
And the white wolf-winter, hungry and frore,
Can prowl the North by a frozen door

[1] *John Brown's Body*, Rinehart & Company, Inc. Copyright 1927, 1928 by Stephen Vincent Benét. Copyright renewed 1955, 1956 by Rosemary Carr Benét.

But here we have fed him on bacon-fat
And he sleeps by the stove like a lazy cat.
Here Christmas stops at everyone's house
With a jug of molasses and green, young boughs,
And the little New Year, the weakling one,
Can lie outdoors in the noonday sun,
Blowing the fluff from a turkey-wing
At skies already haunted with Spring—

Oh Georgia . . . Georgia . . . the careless yield!
The watermelons ripe in the field!
The mist in the bottoms that taste of fever
And the yellow river rolling forever.

Surely everyone everywhere has a special feeling for his home: "This is my own, my native land"; but I believe you will agree with me that, within America, the feeling of patriotism as relevant to a region rather than to the whole of our country is a peculiar mark of the Southerner. In our Civil War, the Federals generally fought for the Union; a Confederate fought for his own state. At its highest level this spirit and motivation are shown in a letter General Robert E. Lee wrote in May, 1861, to a little girl at the North:

It is painful to think how many friends will be separated and estranged by our unhappy disunion. May God reunite our severed bonds of friendship, and turn our hearts to peace! I can say in sincerity that I bear animosity against no one. Wherever the blame may be, the fact is that we are in the midst of a fratricidal war. I must side either with or against my section or country. I cannot raise my hand against my birth-place, my home, my children. I should like, above all things, that our difficulties might be peaceably arranged, and still trust that a merciful God, who I know will not unnecessarily afflict us, may yet allay the fury for war. Whatever may be the result of the contest, I foresee that the country will have to pass through a terrible ordeal, a necessary expiation perhaps for our national sins. May God direct all for our good, and shield and preserve you and yours!

The fury for war was not allayed, and before it passed it fixed upon the South, as a permanent sectional characteristic, a self-consciousness that had been building during the period in which the war approached. The North and the South did not begin their history within the United States with strong feelings of sectionalism. The seeds of future differences, however, were sown in the Convention which framed our Constitution—and even before. The Virginia Convention of May, 1776, instructed its delegates to the Continental Congress at Philadelphia to declare for American independence and to unite with the other colonies, but its instructions added: "Provided, that the power of forming government for, and the regulation of the internal concerns of each colony, be left to their respective colonial legislatures." Thus was the principle of state rights set forth in the very beginning. This principle, carried to its logical conclusion by the disciples of John C. Calhoun (who would rather be logical than right and, therefore, could never be President), brought disunion and civil war. Carried to illogical absurdity within the Confederacy, it helped to wreck what slim chance the South might have had to win its independence.

Sectional consciousness found its first expression in the New England threats of secession in the first decades of the nineteenth century. The prosperity that followed our second war with England, the quick adaptation of the New Englander to the forward impetus of the industrial revolution, and the reaction of the South that expressed itself in the nullification controversy of the 1830's soon fixed the onus of dissatisfaction and self-explanation on the Southern states. These explanations quickly grew into a substantial body of political literature, gradually turned into propaganda for an independent South, and eventually persuaded Southerners that they were something different and that they could be Confederates. Southerners ever since have been reassuring themselves that this was true and self-consciously trying to convert others to the same conclusion—forgetting that the end of the Civil War brought a decision that could not be gainsaid and wrought a *de facto* change in the basis of all of our institutions.

The divergence in literary history, which is a reflection of all other history and which is our best measure of the emotional animus of the past, became apparent (retrospectively at least) in the early development of a kind of indigenous, frontier humor as a special product of Southern authors. Judge A. B. Longstreet was the first and best of the Southern frontier humorists, and his *Georgia Scenes* is a legitimate classic in American literature. This type of humor was not peculiar to the South but became especially well developed there. Likewise, the adventure novel as developed by James Fenimore Cooper was not patented by the North. It had able exponents in the South: John Esten Cooke, John Pendleton Kennedy, William Gilmore Simms, though the Southerners were more likely to claim that they had been influenced by Sir Walter Scott than by Cooper. In their humorous pieces of the first half of the nineteenth century the Southern authors were not self-consciously concerned with their characters as Southerners but only as Americans who were interesting to write about. Cooke, Kennedy, and Simms turned to regional history for their subjects and, unconsciously perhaps, did much to beget a tradition of the "Southern" in literature.

John Esten Cooke is a particular literary friend of mine, not only for what he wrote but also for his very interesting personality. Even so, I enjoy and appreciate the piercing bit of criticism that George W. Bagby, himself a Virginian humorist of note, wrote in 1858. In a piece called "Unkind but Complete Destruction of John Esten Cooke," Bagby commented: "I'm proud of my grand-daddy, proud of the days and deeds of his generation; but I don't want to get so plague-taked proud of him and his times as to undervalue myself and my times. The old times may have been mighty good, but there are some first rate days and prime doings left." Cooke, declared Bagby, was afflicted with a pair of rose-colored goggles of enormous magnifying power. He had, in his novels of colonial Virginia, given the men and women of that period such impeccable characters that Bagby could jibe: "I marvel that such a set of homely, selfish, money-loving cheats and rascals as we are, should have descended from such remarkably fine parents."

Despite such exceptions as Cooke and a few others, who by the 1850's made much of the South as a different region, Southern literature was for a long time very much a part of our stream of national, American literature. Though Edgar Allan Poe charged (and not without reason) that Henry Wadsworth Longfellow and other New Englanders arrogated to themselves the whole field of American letters, we now think of Poe no more as a Southerner than we think of Washington as a Southerner. Poe and Washington were Americans. It was, in fact, by outsiders that the South was established as something different, something different for literary purposes, that is. The Southerner became a distinct character in the novels of Mrs. Caroline Lee Hentz, Robert Montgomery Bird, G. P. R. James, and their ilk.

Slavery and the controversy over it solidified the self-consciousness of the South. The Southern impulse to self-explanation manifested in the halls of Congress, in the pseudo-sociology of the defenders of slavery, and in the daily and weekly papers was also manifested in literary efforts. Yet the most famous and successful work about slavery was not the product of a Southerner but Harriet Beecher Stowe's *Uncle Tom's Cabin*. That whatever chance has ruled my own life has taken me from my birthplace in Washington, Georgia (most Confederate of Georgia towns), almost in the shadow of the home of Robert Toombs, to Brunswick, Maine, and a house within yelling distance of Mrs. Stowe's home at the time she wrote *Uncle Tom's Cabin* is irrelevant to our subject here—but hardly irrelevant to the way I feel about the subject. Mrs. Stowe's book antagonized the South. Without great literary merit, *Uncle Tom's Cabin* was, nevertheless, a book great in its effect. It put the South more than ever on the defensive about its "peculiar institution." It magnified the South's self-consciousness about a facet of Southern life which many Southerners, even then, viewed with strained apology. A score or more answers to Mrs. Stowe's book failed miserably, but tried desperately, to explain slavery and the South.

Concomitant with the development of American literature was the development of the American publishing industry. For a long time American publishing spread itself pretty generally among the major cities: Boston, New York, Philadelphia, Baltimore, Richmond, Charleston. By the middle of the nineteenth century, however, commercial book publishing was concentrated in Boston, New York, and Philadelphia. Rightly or wrongly, Southern authors and ambitious littérateurs felt that this concentration militated against their finding publication.

It is no wonder, then, that the Civil War was greeted as a release from Yankee domination of literature. A Southern editor declared in May, 1861:

The destiny of the South will be but a crude and unfinished attempt, an unmeaning, inconsequential projection into time and space, unless along with her political independence she achieves her independence in thought and education, and in all those forms of mental improvement which . . . are included in literature.

The *Southern Literary Messenger* noted early in the war: "We are about to avail ourselves of the splendid opening which the impending Revolution secures to every Southern enterprise," and Henry Hotze, the Confederate propaganda agent in London wrote in *The Index:*

At present . . . the pen is abandoned for the sword. But when the struggle is over, we are confident the Confederacy will occupy a distinguished position in the Republic of Letters. The life and death conflict for national existence will increase the mental activity of the nation. The spirit and excitement evolved by the war will not subside at the advent of peace. It will then be employed in devoted efforts to promote the prosperity, greatness, and glory of the Confederate States of America; and it will also seek its outlet in literature.

The years of the war were surprisingly productive times for the writers of the South, but they produced little of enduring value. The literary importance of the war is for a different reason.

The Civil War is only a part of the heritage of the modern South, but it is a focal point in that heritage. Those four and a half years from December, 1860, to April, 1865, conditioned the Southern version of the American heritage that had gone before. They conditioned succeeding generations to a sectional interpretation of the continuing heritage.

Appomattox did not produce a new nation, thenceforth and forever indivisible. Appomattox was a bitter defeat for the South. The end of the war brought back to the Union eleven beaten states. After two years of steadily ebbing fortunes the Confederacy had been driven to surrender, but there were few Southerners who would admit error in their course in fighting the war. The Southern states bowed to might; they were not persuaded to a new conviction. Reunion came later. For Southerners Appomattox brought the "bottom rail on top," not the "year of jubilo."

It is easy for the Southerner to remember this, for a decade of Reconstruction added insult to injury. No Marshall Plan, no Point Four Program helped to bring the South back to equality within the nation. The Southerner has heard too frequently and too directly of the struggles of his people for him to forget. He knows differently from other Americans the hardships of war and reconstruction. Misery loves company. But he who has risen from misery wants to make very sure it will never again engulf him. This was the motivation of Scarlett O'Hara. Consciously or unconsciously, it is still a regional motivation.

With its whole effort directed toward war, with war a part of every household, of every life, the Confederate South achieved a unanimity of thought and action the section had never known before and reached a fully defined self-consciousness. Defeat created the solid South, political solidarity, and an even deeper sense of self-consciousness. Alexander H. Stephens retreated into a legalistic, detailed defense of the correctness of a position that force had, rightly or wrongly, made untenable. Other Confederates (with the notable exception of Lee) wrote their own apologia. The Bourbons rose to political domination of Southern thought, trying to reverse the march of history by return to a past that no longer existed. "The victors forget, the vanquished remember," writes Sir Winston Churchill. *The vanquished remember.* All insults, all offenses, all slights, the vanquished South remembered and related to the war. Too often the war became a cloak to cover Southern shortcomings. Too often it was an excuse. *The victors forget.* The war became a part of the American past for the North. The North had the wealth and the power to move on. For a long time the South could honor itself only in defiance and remembrance. The past of the South, for sixty years, became centered in recollection of the war. Men who had been rollicking, randying, roistering soldiers became, in retrospect, knights of a vanished Southern chivalry. Demagogues whose most positive accomplishments had been spitting tobacco juice and shouting became "statesmen of the Old South." Filiopietism replaced patriotism. Apology paraded as history. Confederate self-explanation had full sway—in literature, in history, and in fact.

I speak of the past. But the past is also now. I have talked only of the background. But the background is part of the present. History moves in a continuous stream but is forever backing and filling. The self-consciousness of the modern South is a part of its fabric because the nineteenth-century South wove this self-consciousness into its warp and woof.

The literary South was not too long recovering from the war. A great flowering of Southern letters came in the 1870's and 1880's, not as the work of a school of letters or of any combination of the efforts of associated literary men. Rather, it was a flowering of individual talents: Joel Chandler Harris, Sidney Lanier, Paul Hamilton Hayne, Henry Timrod, George Washington Cable, John Albion Tourgée, and Grace King.

This flowering of Southern literature was not a literary Bourbonism. Though Harris' charming relation of plantation folk stories fed the Bourbon idea of the South, he wrote for the nation and was convinced that a writer's view should be national. Cable enraged his contemporaries with his penetrating, devastating portrayal of the New Orleans Creoles and his espousal of the cause of the Negro. "It is," he wrote, "an insult to a forebearing God and the civilized world for us to sit in full view of moral and civil wrongs manifestly bad and curable, saying that we must expect this or that, and that, geologically considered, we are getting along quite rapidly." (Had the phrase "with all deliberate speed" been current in his day, Cable would doubtless have used it.) The literary hero of Bourbonism was the young Henry Grady whose New South idea was a bastard kind of New Englandism, transplanted to restore a South of the past to Southerners of the past. Grady's sincerity as a Southerner cannot be doubted, but he bestowed on his region a philosophy that was the ideological counterpart of freight-rate discrimination and of the South as a sort of colonial fetter to the rest of the nation. Fortunately he has been placed in proper historical perspective by Vann Woodward.

It is difficult to say to what extent escape from the reality of defeat and the harshness of living in a land defeated and isolated figured in the rise of the local colorists of Southern literary history. There must have been a connection. It would be many years after the war before Southerners would write objectively, impassively, of it. In the meantime the writings of Harris, Thomas Nelson Page, Mary Noailles Murfree, James Lane Allen, and Kate Chopin gave a series of accounts of what was different in pockets of Southern culture and emphasized the South and Southerners as different from the rest of America and the rest of Americans. Perhaps this was escapism; perhaps it represented a feeling on the part of postwar Southerners that their views of America as a whole were unwelcome and that their talents—very considerable talents —could be exercised only in this restricted measure. In any case, the very worth of their literary efforts, extolling the local and the very Southern, added to the impression of the Southerner as the ultra–self-conscious individual, explaining his own region at the drop of an aspersion and condemned to perpetual self-justification.

Much of the same happened in the field of history—with perhaps more reason. As in any war, the victors were the first to interpret the Civil War as history. Confederates who achieved publication did so mostly with autobiographies or highly personalized historical accounts. Textbooks and formal histories were the products of the North and were not always without prejudice. It was the turn of the century before this pattern was no longer so overwhelming that Southerners felt they had to overstate whenever they had any opportunity whatever to tell their side of history.

The old antipathies died slowly, but a new breed of realism appeared in the novels of Mary Johnston, Ellen Glasgow, and James Boyd. Finally the history of the war was subjected to treatment by the revisionists of both North and South.

Personal journalism is a prized American tradition, now too often honored in the breach. Fortunately we remember the best of personal journalism and not the vituperation that frequently marred it. But the South was lucky in its famous editors: E. A. Pollard of Richmond, Francis Warrington Dawson of Charleston, Walter Hines Page of Raleigh, Henry Watterson of Louisville, Henry Grady of Atlanta (who was a better editor than sociologist)—to name a few. These men too were spokesmen of the self-conscious South.

I speak of the present as well as the past. As Southerners we are still self-conscious. But we make more and more breakthroughs into being Americans. Thomas Wolfe, DuBose Heyward, Stark Young, Evelyn Scott—these are Americans. Despite a plethora (particularly during our years of the Civil War Centennial) of amateur, pietistic historians, we have our share of real historians too: Woodward, Frank Vandiver, Bell Wiley, and others. Howard Odum, W. J. Cash, Clarence Nixon, and other sociologists have defined the South as a region not a section. Ralph McGill and Hodding Carter are spokesmen for a really new South, not apologists for an era gone with the wind. Tennessee Williams, Eudora Welty, Caroline Gordon, the late William Faulkner (despite his private, inner civil war on the race question) serve as interpreters of their region. They are American writers of Southern background, not twentieth-century local-colorists.

Let it be so. Let the South bury its self-consciousness as John Esten Cooke buried his silver spurs in a futile but appropriate *beau geste*—on the battlefield of Appomattox. Let us move, not futilely but more than ever appropriately, to being Americans as well as Southerners.

LOUIS D. RUBIN, JR.

Notes on a Rear-Guard Action

IT IS SAID of General Robert Toombs that he never conceded, and that when the news of the great Chicago fire reached the state of Georgia, the General went down to the telegraph office to find out about it. Afterward he was asked whether he had any late reports, and he replied that all possible protective measures were being taken to prevent the spread of the flames, "but the wind is in our favor."

Toombs's remark was widely and gleefully repeated by his delighted fellow citizens, and we still rather enjoy it, because of its invincible belligerency. The fact is, however, that much of its humor comes because even by 1871 it was so very quixotic, denying as it did that the war was over. Barely six years after Appomattox Court House, the South had all but unanimously conceded that the war was both over and lost, that Chicago was not an enemy city any more, and that the South was once more and forever part of one nation indivisible. Except in the matter of race relations, it has generally been acting on that premise ever since. Even there it has been coming around recently; the flare-up in Mississippi was an ugly and abortive protest, doomed to failure. South Carolina was much more sensible about the matter; loudly did its leaders vow resistance and loudly did its daily press trumpet defiance, but when the moment of truth came, law and order prevailed at Clemson College.

I wish I could attribute South Carolina's good manners entirely to idealistic motives, but I am of two minds about it. It was partly a matter of not wanting anything unpleasant to take place, because it would be bad publicity and might interfere with plans for industrial development. It is well known that industrial concerns do not set up new plants where there is widespread disorder and violence, and ever since Henry Grady's day the South has most of all been concerned with attracting industry. By and large it has been doing a pretty good job of it; the money has

LOUIS D. RUBIN, JR., Professor of English, Hollins College, has long had an interest in Southern literature as both art and history. A distinguished practicing novelist, Professor Rubin is also a literary critic whose telling comments are widely published.

come South, the factories have sprung up everywhere, and no longer is the South a colony of the Northeast. With the money has come payrolls, and with payrolls have come schools, and with schools has come, however unequally, education. "Educate a nigger," I believe the motto used to be, "and you spoil a good farm hand." This is precisely what has happened. When you teach a colored man to read, you can't be sure that he will read only the instruction manual that comes with his employer's tractor. He might read the U.S. Constitution and, unless he has been properly warned off, he might even start believing it, and if that happens, there is no telling what will follow.

This is what went wrong in Mississippi, it seems to me. That Southern state tried to have it both ways. For many decades Mississippi paid very little attention to what was being said about the need for industry and payrolls, and went right on raising cotton. It was thus enabled, at least in part, to retain the kind of society that existed before the Industrial Revolution. But we know what happened to cotton after World War I; finally even Mississippi decided it had to industrialize. Two decades ago Mississippi embarked on what was known as the BAWI program: Balance Agriculture with Industry. I quote from an article by the director of agricultural and industrial development for the state in a 1953 publication entitled *Today's South:*

> Mississippi, steeped in the mellow tradition and romantic history of the colorful bygone era of the Old South, is today undergoing an industrial and agricultural revolution which is attracting national attention.
>
> A widely accepted program to "balance agriculture with industry" has passed after more than a decade from the experimental state into a time-tested formula for helping cure the state's economic ills.
>
> Today BAWI, as it is called, is paying off in employment and payrolls and in markets for the state's abundant natural resources.[1]

Unfortunately for those who would have it otherwise, the state of Mississippi found what other Southern states had also discovered, that you can't do that sort of thing and expect the people who are affected by it not to change, colored people as well as whites. Education is a very pernicious thing. The result was what happened at Oxford. By that time it was too late to go back and repeal the BAWI plan; the damage was done. The director of development's article, it seems to me, was quite prophetic; the industrial and agricultural revolution in Mississippi did indeed attract national attention, though not quite in the way that the state of Mississippi intended.

Oxford was in the news twice in 1962. On two separate occasions,

---

[1] William E. Barksdale, " 'BAWI' Program Attracts Industry,' in "Today's South," *Editor and Publisher*, October 31, 1953, p. 89.

stories bearing its dateline were read throughout the world. One, of course, was the Meredith incident. The other, back in the summer, was the death of William Faulkner. The Meredith incident attracted the greater attention, perhaps, but I daresay that the death of the novelist will be remembered when the Meredith incident has been forgotten.

It will be so because the death of Faulkner is a great symbolic milestone in a momentous historical process that has been going on for a century, while the Meredith incident is only a momentary annoyance, which in the history books of the future will at most merit only a single sentence in a long chapter. The chapter will be entitled, "The End of the Old South." It will chronicle an American region's gradual absorption into the mainstream of American history. Most of the factual data is already in; the larger meaning is and has long since been apparent; the result is foregone. There is nothing that can change it now.

What do the death of William Faulkner and the admission of James Meredith into the student body of the University of Mississippi have in common? To the mobs of people who congregated about that campus, the thousands of United States Army troops who stood guard there, the newspaper and magazine reporters who came from all over the world to cover the story, there was no apparent connection. Relatively few of them had ever heard of William Faulkner. Those who had were doubtless too busy to think about him. Yet all the same, there was a relationship. For the novels of William Faulkner and the events that took place on the campus of the University of Mississippi last fall were part and parcel of the same historical happenstance.

Faulkner was but one—the foremost, the greatest—of a number of talented novelists and poets who were born in the South about the turn of the century, and who came into prominence during the 1920's and 1930's. The noteworthy thing about these writers, so far as the South was concerned, was that they were almost the first group of distinguished writers to come from the South. The nineteenth-century South produced almost no writers of major stature, with the possible exception of Edgar Allan Poe. Compared with Melville, Hawthorne, Whitman, Thoreau, Emerson, Dickinson, James, what are Sidney Lanier, Joel Chandler Harris, George Washington Cable, Henry Timrod, William Gilmore Simms, Thomas Nelson Page, Paul Hamilton Hayne? There is only Mark Twain, if we may claim him. H. L. Mencken, in the year 1920, wrote that so far as the fine arts were concerned, the South was a veritable Sahara of the Bozart. Who was to say him nay? Of course he exaggerated; Ellen Glasgow and James Branch Cabell were already publishing good work, but it was not until the decade after World War I that anyone took them very seriously. It was the twenties before there suddenly began to appear people in the South who could write books that people in the North and the West and in Europe might notice. And when they began to appear, they came almost at once, and in great number and brilliance. The novels, stories, and poems written by William Faulkner, Thomas Wolfe, Robert Penn Warren, Katherine Anne Porter, Eudora Welty, Erskine Caldwell, John Crowe Ransom, Allen Tate, Carson McCullers, Andrew Lytle, and others have attracted world-wide attention; it is impossible to judge the achievement of American literature during the decades after World War I without considering their work. They are in the mainstream. They dominate the scene.

What happened in the South that might cause this? This is a problem to which I have addressed myself on several occasions in the past. I shall not go into it now at any great length.[2] Suffice it to say that when a society undergoes great change, when its attitudes, its values, its patterns are violently disrupted, those of its citizens who have literary talents, which is to say the kind of imagination that seeks to give experience an order and meaning through words and images, may well find it difficult or impossible to discover such order in their daily lives, and so may seek to create the order in stories and poems. Elizabethan England, moving from feudalism into mercantilism, was such a community; so was late nineteenth- and early twentieth-century Ireland; so was late nineteenth-century Russia; and so on. I do not insist that this is the only condition needed for a literary flowering, but it is certainly an important condition.

Now the Civil War, whatever its other effects on American life, served greatly to retard and postpone the impact of nineteenth-century industrialism on the Southern states; for one thing it all but destroyed the region's capital wealth, without which industrial development was impossible. When at last industrialism did come, however, it came swiftly and violently, with consequent great impact on what had been a rural, contained, agricultural society. To the generation of Southerners growing up in the early 1900's, the discrepancy between what they were taught to believe and what they saw all around them; between notions of truth, beauty, goodness, caste, class, conviction as enunciated by one's elders in home, church, and school, and the actual conditions of experience—the discrepancy between what should be and what actually was—must have been most puzzling.

No one knows exactly what it is that makes a man into a writer. I

[2] See "The South and the Faraway Country," *Virginia Quarterly Review*, Summer, 1962, pp. 444–59; and "Southern Literature: The Historical Image," in Louis D. Rubin, Jr., and Robert D. Jacobs (eds.), *South: Modern Southern Literature in Its Cultural Setting* (New York, 1961), pp. 29–47. Perhaps the best essay on this subject is Allen Tate's "The Profession of Letters in the South," in *On the Limits of Poetry* (New York, 1948), pp. 265–81.

sometimes think it has something to do with a kind of masochism, together with an almost pathological desire for self-exposure. Allen Tate's description of Emily Dickinson I sometimes think is a word picture of all good novelists and poets: "Her poetry is a magnificent personal confession, blasphemous and, in its self-revelation, its honesty, almost obscene." In any event, the literary impulse, as I have suggested, surely has to do with a compulsion to give order and form to, or more accurately to discover them in, an experience that in real life seems not to possess sufficient pattern and logic. And of course a part of that experience is one's own self.

What I am suggesting is what many others have also suggested: that the so-called Southern Literary Renascence, that outburst of distinguished writing after World War I in a region hitherto bereft of literary achievement by its citizens, may be directly attributed to what Mr. Barksdale was talking about in his article on the BAWI plan—the fact that the Old South, steeped in tradition and historical loyalties, was undergoing a social revolution. What Southerners had considered to be eternal and unchanging truth was both changing and dubious. And its writers were quick to discover this, for indeed, it was abundantly present within their own minds and hearts.

Now all this is well and good, but it will not be worth saying unless it is clearly understood that it is *novelists* and *poets* that we are talking about, and not social scientists. For these men and women are artists, and their response to the change within their society—a change, I repeat, existing within themselves—was that of art. They did not sit down and ask themselves, "How can I best illustrate the change in values going on in today's South?" They did not even think of such things at all, or if they did, it was not as writers, but as ordinary citizens did, as journalists, as pamphleteers, as businessmen, as politicians. Instead they thought of people, places, situations, which they made into characters, scenes, and plots. Any writer is primarily interested in people, usually himself. He writes a novel about people. His object is to show the way people are, which is to say, the way the world is. And if a novel is a good novel, it will do this with much perception, so that other people, reading the novel, recognize the truth of what the author is saying about people. The reader already knew it, but he didn't realize he knew it, and he didn't know it nearly so forcibly, until he was exposed to the novel.

Novelists, then, write about people, not political and social problems, and the humanness of their novels is what counts. But novelists are not just people; they are people of a particular time and place, and what they know is themselves in that time and place. The time and place known to the novelists I have been talking about was the twentieth-century South.

They grew up in it, among Southerners, with Southern loyalties, Southern ties, Southern attitudes; they met the modern world. They observed the ways of modernity through Southern eyes, and at the same time they judged the institutions, customs, and habits of the South not through the tradition, but as moderns. It was, in other words, a time of mid-passage.

Since they were Southerners, since the South and Southerners were what they knew, they wrote Southern books. I do not mean by this that they necessarily wrote "about" Southerners living in the South; rather, the kind of fictional world they created was one that took its lineaments from the Southern world they knew, and the concerns of the fictional characters they created were the concerns of Southerners. They tended to see life on the terms that their experience as Southerners presented itself. This was manifested in the way they used language, in the kinds of problems of human definition that they thought important, in what they thought men were and what they thought men ought to be. These things being so, then, it ought to be possible for one to read their novels and poems, keeping in mind at all times that they *are* novels and poems and not social studies, in order to find out things about the South. And so I think it is.

I want to stress at this point, however, that it is one thing for a book to be "Southern," which is to say that it reflects and embodies Southern experience, and quite another for it to be "about" the South. Not all "Southern" books are about the South; for example, Katherine Anne Porter's *Ship of Fools* is not about the South, yet it is a "Southern" novel. By this I mean that the way that Miss Porter looks at human beings, the things she thinks are important about them, the values by which she judges their conduct, are quite "Southern," even though none of the major characters is Southern, and indeed most of them are not even Americans. Contrariwise, it is obvious that a play such as Jean Paul Sartre's *La putain respecteuse* is "about" the South, but it is in no way Southern. We are not talking about subject matter when we say that a novel or a poem is Southern; we are talking about the way that the book is written and what it shows.

But it is not enough to stop here. We must make a further, perhaps more difficult, point: not only are books such as *Ship of Fools* not "about" the South, which is obvious, but, in a very important way, neither are books such as *Light in August* or *Look Homeward, Angel* "about" the South. This may seem strange; you might well ask, for example, how any book could be more nearly "about" the South than *Light in August*. Does not Faulkner set his novel in Mississippi? Does he not deal with the problem of whether a man is or is not a Negro, and what this means if he is so? Are not all the incidents those which are associated with the South? There is a lynching, the Civil War and Reconstruction are mentioned, there are Negroes and whites, tenant farming, sawmill operations, a country store, moonshining, and so on. What does it mean to say that such a novel as this is not "about" the South?

What I mean is simply this: there is no important attempt on the part of the author to make "real life" observations about the South. He was not interested in giving an account of typical life in Mississippi. His object was not to write a guidebook to that state, nor was it to make a political or sociological observation on the treatment of Negroes in Mississippi. He was not, that is, either historian or journalist, sociologist or psychiatrist. He was an artist, a novelist, and *Light in August* is not a treatise, but a tragedy. The laws which govern its characters' behavior, the meaning of the situations in which they find themselves, the outcome of those situations, are those of art, not those of journalism or social science.

Now it is precisely this matter that causes so much difficulty in the average person's comprehension of Faulkner, or for that matter of much additional Southern writing. Why, the question is so often asked, did Faulkner insist on portraying all Southerners as sadists, lynchers, nymphomaniacs, murderers, perverts, criminals, thieves, adulterers, miscegenists, racists, and so forth? Why didn't he show Southern life as it really is? Most Southerners aren't like that; not even most Mississippians are like that. Why did Faulkner malign his native region so consistently? Why did he continually write about all that violence and murder and filth?

You have all heard that question asked. And indeed, when one talks with people who do not know the South and is appalled to find that many of them *do* believe that Faulkner is describing typical Southern life, one has a certain sympathy for this objection. One can almost—though not quite—understand why, when Faulkner was awarded the Nobel Prize for literature, the editor of his native state's leading newspaper deplored the award and declared indignantly that Faulkner "is a propagandist of degradation and belongs in the privy school of literature." Admittedly it isn't very good advertising, though perhaps what took place at Oxford in the fall of 1962 makes the offense seem unimportant.

Yet however much we may sympathize with the objection, however much we may deplore the way in which so many people insist on reading not only Faulkner's novels but those of most other Southern authors as well, there is no real justification for blaming Faulkner for it. One cannot hold him responsible for the misuse of his novels. One can no more blame Faulkner for misrepresenting life in Mississippi than one can blame Shakespeare for misrepresenting life in England, or Sophocles for misrepresenting life in Thebes. Neither of the three was engaged in writing journalism; they were writing tragedies. Their object was not the representation of typical everyday human conduct; they were trying to show what certain men were like and thus what life is like, and to do this they were engaged in describing experience in its ultimate dimensions, those of life and death, heroism and suffering, bravery and cowardice, love and hatred.

So that if we want to discuss Faulkner and the South, or Wolfe, or Warren or any good Southern writer, we must remember that there is no intent on the author's part to give a journalistically authentic portrayal of Southern life. We must not read *Light in August* as if it were an explanation of why Negroes get lynched in Mississippi. In that respect it will prove very flimsy documentation. What *Light in August* has to tell us about the South is something else than that.

The central character of *Light in August* is a man named Joe Christmas who thinks he is part Negro though there is no real evidence that he is. Joe Christmas lives in a shed behind the house of a white woman, Joanna Burden, and at night he sleeps with her. At length she tries to kill him, but her pistol misfires, and he slays her instead. He flees, is hunted down, jailed, breaks free, and a posse corners him and shoots him to death. As he lies dying he is mutilated by one of the pursuers.

This is assuredly a very violent incident, not at all pleasant. Yet one cannot object to it as being in any way gratuitous violence. It is dramatically appropriate, the only kind of end which can properly come to Joe Christmas. It is almost as though it was what Joe Christmas wished to happen. What gives the novel its meaning is *why* Joe wished it to happen, which has to do with what kind of person Joe Christmas is. And what the novel has to tell us about the South depends upon our understanding of why Joe Christmas came to the end he did.

The key to Joe Christmas' death lies in his life. Born illegitimately to a mother who died, he is taken to an orphanage where, perhaps because of his dark complexion—his father may not have been a Negro, but if not he was evidently a Mexican or a Spaniard with a dark skin—he is taunted by his playmates with accusations of "nigger!" and his sense of guilt and punishment is seriously shocked when he is bribed by a female hospital attendant when he thinks he has done wrong. This confusion of punishment is further intensified when he is adopted by foster parents who are fanatical Calvinists and who punish him brutally under the guise of inculcating justice and goodness in him. His doubt about his Negro ancestry continues to plague him so that, as the result of these and other incidents, he grows to manhood unable to accept love, and tormented by his failure to know who he is, something he must know if he is ever to find his rightful place in society. The result is that he embarks on a long career of violence and brutality, culminating in his liaison with Joanna Burden. When this mutually destructive relationship ends, he goes almost willingly to his death.

This is but one, though the most important, of a number of closely interrelated sequences in the novel. What it depicts is the quest of a man to find out who he is. Joe Christmas does not know whether he is white or black, and he inhabits a society in which one must be either one or the other. The important point is that Joe *could*, so far as the society is concerned, pass as either. Indeed, he has at times lived in both guises. The problem then is one within himself. He needs certainty, he needs to be able to define himself as a man, and because of his upbringing he is unable to accept the limitations or the advantages of either choice. He rages against the need to assume an identity in society; his response to human limitation is violence. When even the ultimate violence he can commit, the ultimate blasphemy and rejection he can utter, fail to tell him who he is, fail to evoke an absolute standard by which he can measure himself, he chooses the only certainty still left to him: his own destruction.

Now what does this tell us about the South? It tells us, I think, that man needs to know who he is and what he is, and that a society in which men are fitted into roles which fail to allow them to define themselves fully as human beings must be a society of unrest, of violence, of suffering. But of course that is no revelation, is it? Don't the social scientists show us that, and in much more documentary fashion?

No, they do not. They don't show it to us; they tell it to us, by means of statistics, case histories, factual data. What Faulkner does in *Light in August* is to show us what it means to be a human being and not to know who one is and is not, to confront society and to try to live both without and within it, when one can do neither except at the expense of one's own identity. He shows us what it means, because he dramatizes it as a tragedy in which Joe Christmas, through not knowing how to be human and not being allowed to be himself, can find surcease only in self-destruction.

So that if we read this novel, and accept what it has to tell us, we will know, in a way that no non-fictional account, no sociological or journalistic analysis can tell us, the human meaning of racism—and not only that, but of all ways of treating human beings as less than human. With due reservation and skepticism as to the difficulty and even the absurdity of attempting to order one's life through works of art, I cannot conceive how anyone could read *Light in August* and ever feel quite the same about Negroes.

Of course I realize that in so saying, I may seem to have contradicted my original point, which was that a book such as *Light in August* is not "about" the South at all. And it is not: for the object of Faulkner in writing it was not to tell his readers about the South. Joe Christmas is not the "average" Southern Negro or even a portrait of a typical victim of a lynch mob. He is not, one is glad to say, a "typical" human being at all—for most human beings do not do the violent things that he did. He is an exaggeration, a tragic hero. Yet it is in his very exaggeration, his outlandish proportions, the intensity of his grief and fears and pains and desires, that he speaks most directly to us. By pursuing Joe Christmas' human dimensions to their ultimate proportions Faulkner is able to dramatize that humanness, to show it to us clean, unflawed by compromise or qualification. He shows us, that is, what it means to be a human being, and we recognize in this pervert, this murderer, this criminal, what is also present in ourselves. And since Joe Christmas is a Negro, or thinks he is, we can see that a Negro is a human being and what it must be like, again extended to the ultimate dimensions of tragedy, to try to be both human and Negro.

This is not something that can be measured. It cannot be transferred into the particulars of daily life, to serve as a guide to the improvement of race relations, to the sociology of rural Mississippi. It is not an attempt to describe the way things are in Mississippi. Thus it is not "about" Mississippi or the South. Yet the human insight it contains, the truth it has to tell us about compassion and cruelty and pride, speak powerfully to the concerns of Mississippi and the South today.

For it is the nature of the Southern experience today that the large and elemental passions are in the news, at the surface of experience. We are assailed, in a most dramatic fashion, with human problems the most complex, the most urgent to solve. And it is impossible for us to look at these problems sideways. Caught up in the rending process of transition, we are brought face to face with events that possess instant and inescapable meaning. All our old loyalties, our historical attitudes, our instinctive responses, are up for examination. The compromises we have habitually relied upon to square conflicts between our ideas of the good and our knowledge of the imperfect ordering of our society are one after the other proving unsatisfactory.

I think we always knew, in the South, that we were not doing right by the Negro. But we also knew how very hard and how inconvenient it would be to do what was right. Both the right and the difficulty of doing right were very sharp realities, and we could not ignore their existence. So we worked out, as all human beings would naturally do, some very elaborate compromises with our integrity, and we persuaded ourselves that these would suffice. So they did, for a long time. But that time began running out on us many decades ago, and what we have been doing for the most part is trying to find new compromises and to beat a kind of grudging and dignified retreat. We have been waging a rear-guard action; we have been trying to keep the process of change from overwhelming us, while we were getting to where we had to go. I remember when I was a child, for example, that colored people, when mentioned in my hometown newspaper, were never called Mr. or Mrs. It was a little mark of indignity, part of a pattern of behavior. Nowadays this is no longer so; again, a small thing to be sure, but a sign that we are accommodating ourselves to the notion that Negroes are fully human beings after all. We have given up that line of defense and have retreated to new, prepared positions. Soon we shall give those up, and keep right on retreating. We shall keep retreating until, finally, one day, there is no place else left to retreat, and to our amazement we will discover that the war is over. It will be over because there won't be anything left to fight about.

I do not want to minimize the ugliness and the discomfort of this rear-guard action. It is a discomforting business, and as events in Mississippi and more recently in Alabama showed, a very ugly one. Military historians would tell us, I believe, that rear-guard actions are among the most bitter of military operations. They are sullen, dogged, vicious affairs, with sporadic flares of violence and travail. Each battle, each engagement, is a repetition of the previous one. If one were to compile an anthology on historical principles of the defenses proposed by Southern spokesmen against justice for the Negro, beginning back in the 1830's and 1840's and continuing up to the present, what would be most appalling and most disconcerting to our pride would be the monotony, the sameness, of it all. We used the same arguments, with only minor adjustments for particular issues, against Daniel Webster and Abraham Lincoln that we have used against Earl Warren. (This is one reason, I suspect, why most of the professional historians that I know are opposed to segregation; they know how shopworn and unoriginal the arguments used in its favor are.) We go right on battling: against emancipation, against voting rights, against educational equality, against housing desegregation, against desegregated lunch counters, against integration of public transportation, against desegregation of theaters and libraries —I understand that they have now reopened the library in Albany, Georgia, but have removed all the chairs—and so on. Think of it: a rear-guard action of more than a century's duration, fought as if each engagement were the only one that mattered!

This is what we have had to live with in the South for many decades, and I suppose it will go on for awhile yet. There is no use pretending that it has been very noble or very beautiful. It has been an ugly business, and it has marked all of us. It has consumed a great deal of time and energy that might better have gone into more productive activities. Furthermore, it has had the effect of diverting our attention from much more important things that have been taking place during much of that time. William Styron, who to my mind is the most distinguished Southern writer to have come on the scene since World War II, remarked in an interview recently, when asked whether he thought that the South was changing, that his home town of Hampton, Virginia, now looked like Bridgeport, Connecticut, and it had not looked like that when he was growing up there. If that meant change, he said, then the South had changed greatly. Of course it means change; of course the South has been changing. The whole pattern of Southern life has been transformed by the industrial revolution. To my mind this is of crucial importance. Yet we have paid comparatively little attention to it; we have undertaken no coherent and extended critique of what we have been about these many decades.

Now you may say that this has been an inevitable change, and I would certainly agree. You may even say that it is, taken all in all, more desirable than not, and again I think I would agree. But the point is that we have let it take place haphazardly, willy-nilly; we have done little or nothing to control it, to see that it is done at the minimum cost to what we should like to retain in Southern life. I cannot but feel that we might have done a better job of industrializing and urbanizing than we have done. If you drive through downtown Richmond, Virginia, today you will find that all the historic dignity and beauty of that handsome city has been ripped out and destroyed. Was that necessary? Did Richmond have to pay that price for its industrialization?

Let me propose another example. We champion the sacrosanctity of our public schools. We assert that to allow Negro students to enrol in our white schools would destroy those schools. Yet while we have been massively resisting federal tyranny, and expending all our energies in a futile attempt to keep those schools lily white, what has been happening? The quality of Southern public school education has gone rapidly downhill. The corps of dedicated professional men and women who taught me in elementary and high school, citizens for whom teaching was an honorable and rewarding career, is gone. With some notable exceptions, the caliber, the quality of persons teaching in public schools has steadily declined. We have let this happen! We have been expending all our energies on keeping Negroes out of the schools, instead of working to improve those schools. Think of the difference in the attitude you had toward public school teachers in your community thirty years ago, and your present attitude. Do you still consider the high-school teacher the distinguished citizen that you once did, a quarter-century ago? You do not. Allowing for exaggeration, he is now a moderately well-paid clerk.

This might have been prevented, had we thought about the problem. Had we spent the last quarter-century worrying, not about how to keep qualified Negroes out of our schools, but about what we could do to maintain and enhance the educational quality of our schools, how we could secure and keep first-class teachers; had we expended the same amount of emotional energy and intellect and money in improving our schools that we expended in our traditional rear-guard action; how changed our schools and our community might now be, and all for the better. As it is, we will still have the integrated schools, and neither the white nor the Negro students will get a very good education in them. To paraphase the Irish poet, behold this proof of Southern sense.

But of course that is a utopian dream. People do not behave like that. They go on fighting their rear-guard actions, dealing with immediate events, never worrying about underlying causes, refusing to learn from the past or to face the future. The historians look at the record of what they said and did, trace out the causes and effects, point to patterns, directions, motivations. How can there be doubt as to what has taken place in the South, and what will take place? Barring international calamity or collision of planets, the outcome, the century-long direction, is as certain and as predictable as any problem in applied science. Even those who lead the resistance to any such accommodation to the inevitable privately concede the futility of their opposition. Of course it's a lost cause, declares a friend of mine in private. Yet he is a brilliant and prominent newspaper editor who goes to work each morning and composes vigorous editorials urging his fellow Southerners never to surrender, to stand fast. To persist in the face of defeat, to remain defiant to the bitter end, we call this bravery. And it is, of a sort. Yet sometimes I wonder whether it would not require more bravery than that even to act on the basis of one's reason and wisdom, though one's emotions and one's sense of the state of public opinion urge the suppression of what one knows to be true. It is hard to say. There is always that which is glamorous and enticing about a rear-guard action. How much more appealing is General Toombs's postwar attitude than that of General Longstreet. All the same, it was Longstreet who faced up to what had happened at Appomattox Court House. The South admired Toombs's attitude, and it pronounced Longstreet a turncoat, even while assiduously following the course of action Longstreet took. I fear that it is not very respectable to be a prophet of the inevitable.

Yet, of course, reason does prevail. It has prevailed in Texas. It prevailed recently in South Carolina. They might, at Clemson College, have chosen the path of Mississippi, but they did not. They were wise enough to see that a skirmish would serve no useful purpose. They had the example of Mississippi before them. I can read the sentence that will appear in tomorrow's history books; perhaps Professor Tindall has already composed it. It will be something like this: "Similar bloodshed was avoided in South Carolina early the next year, however, when leaders of that state, realizing the harm that an outbreak of violence might do to civic peace and the state's efforts to attract large-scale industry within its borders, saw to it that the enrolment of a Negro architectural student at Clemson College was accomplished without incident."

Cooler heads prevailed. In Mississippi they did not. In Mississippi there was bluster, passion, violence. The mobs formed about the university; they fired shots into windows. People were killed; others were wounded. And while it was all taking place, over in the cemetery east of town there lay the body of a novelist who had died the summer before. I wondered, as I read the news stories last fall, what he would have done during that crisis if he had been alive. I think perhaps he would have put on his coat and tie and hat and gone on over to the campus, and stood quietly alongside of James Meredith.

Would it have made any difference? I doubt it. Most of the citizens who milled about the campus would not have known who he was, or if they had, they would not have cared. Who was William Faulkner to them?

He was, let us admit it, a utopian. His solution to the problems of the South was absurdly simple and entirely impractical. It is found in *Light in August* and every other one of his novels. It was, Love. That is the great theme of Faulkner: the failure of human love, the tragedy caused by its absence. He looked at the life he knew and saw its misery, its torment, its ugliness, and in every case the reason he found for the presence of misery, torment, and ugliness was the same: the failure of love. Joe Christmas is sadist, pervert, murderer; ultimately he is murdered by another sadist and pervert. Joe Christmas is these things, his murderer is these things, because there was no love, because what love there was distorted, selfish.

Had there been love, had love been stronger than fear, then Joe Christmas would not have been sent forth inexorably on his path of violence. It is the same in all his other novels. In *The Sound and the Fury*, a dynasty collapses, a young man kills himself, a young woman destroys her integrity, an idiot is gelded, lives are ruined, warped, twisted, because there is no love. In *Absalom, Absalom!* a brother kills his brother, a woman goes childless, a man's plans for family and dynasty crumble, because what is sought is sought without love. And so on, in every one of Faulkner's tales.

He wanted the world to be a place where love is stronger than fear, compassion is stronger than hate. It was not such a world, and so he composed tragedies, showing what happened to people when love was absent. He showed the destructiveness of hate, the futility of selfishness, the viciousness of fear. He created human beings dominated by these passions, showed the ruin they wreaked.

His too was a rear-guard action. And in one sense I see all the great writers of the modern South as engaging in just such a rear-guard action. They wrote their novels and poems about human beings caught in a life of confusion, violence, change, people seeking to keep their integrity, to prevent themselves from being immersed in the chaos of time and transition. Examine the fictional worlds they created, the situations they made for their characters: in each instance it is love that mattered most, causing pain and destruction when not present, joy and triumph when realized. For that is mostly what literature is about.

If peace prevails in the South, and it will, if our region is ever to be a place where human beings strive to help other human beings instead of hurting them, then our novelists and our poets will be the prophets of such a time. For in their novels and poems they have all been saying one thing, however utopian, however impractical: each man is a human being. Treat him that way. Nothing else will do. Whether he is black or white, rich or poor, there is no other way. Until that is done, neither the South nor the nation nor the world will ever know peace. Such is the language of Southern literature.

FRANK E. VANDIVER

The Southerner as Extremist

SOUTHERNERS are, and have been, portrayed in various guises: arrogant, cheroot-puffing planters, sipping juleps; power-sodden, leisure-ridden fops, watching in slack-jawed pleasure the beating of a slave; dirt-grubbing sharecroppers, hating their debts to the country store; anonymous amalgams of men, faceless and pale behind their sheets, burning crosses, lynching fellow men; money-worshipping scalawags, grasping the trough of the Great Barbecue; gross politicos, bellowing racist catechisms with Bilbo-like fervor; indignant men of liberal stripe, the James Petigrus, the Hodding Carters, the Ralph McGills, fighting lonely, dirty battles; masses with hate-contorted faces, screaming at television cameras, frothing on schoolyards in Little Rock, New Orleans, Oxford.

No matter the guise, one underrunning trait brands them all: violence. Far back in the history of the South visitors and natives alike noted a violent strain as an integral part of Southern character. "Wild justice easily degenerates into lawless violence," one observer noted in the 1850's, adding that a "bloodthirsty ferocity is developed among the ruder members of the community."

The gentry, however, were by no means immune to extremism. No other part of the country sported as many devotees of the code duello and its attendant protocols of chivalry. Real and fancied sallies against a man's honor required satisfaction, and a quick pistol or deft foil guaranteed an unsmirched reputation. True dandies might boast several victims—pinked if not dispatched. Such personal redress of grievances re-

FRANK E. VANDIVER, Professor of History at Rice University, is presently serving as Harmsworth Professor of American History at Oxford University. An authority on the Confederacy, Professor Vandiver is the author of *Mighty Stonewall, Rebel Brass*, and other studies in Southern history and is currently doing research on General John J. Pershing. This essay was originally delivered on February 28, 1963, as one of a series of lectures on "Extremes in American Life" presented at the University of Judaism in Los Angeles. At the special request of the Rice University Semicentennial Publications Committee, and with the kind permission of Dean Max Vorspan of the University of Judaism, it has been reproduced in this volume.

ceived the blessing of custom well into the first half of the nineteenth century. Southerners regarded individual bravery as part of a man.

Bravery and physical courage came to be so vital a part of the "Southern way of life" that they were paraded at every opportunity. Where legitimate opportunities were scarce, special ones were often staged for displays of bravado and derring-do. Tournaments of a medieval character were sometimes held, with balanced cavaliers atop Arabian chargers doing battle for a lady's favor.

Such belligerent courage, such bellicose honor, can easily warp into senseless bullying, given the proper circumstances. The proper circumstances existed in the South. A frontier civilization which grew in waves of westward settlement, the South developed a rustic cast reinforced by abundant, thinly settled land. Rustics are normally fiercely independent, industrious folk, jealous of rights and chattels. Southerners had all these traits, but they were conditioned by one constant peculiar to the South: slavery. The slave system in its economic, political, and social implications added an intangible something to the violent strain running strong in Southerners.

Although the traditional idealization of Dixie as a happy land of moonlight, magnolias, and jollifying pickaninnies has faded before history, there is some truth in it. And there is some truth, too, in the other side of the idyl—the side of misery, fear, and Simon Legree. Power does indeed corrupt and never so surely as when exercised directly over men. Slaves were at the mercy of their masters, and while some Southern states boasted legal limits to an owner's authority, in practice he could do almost as he wished with his property. Weak men, prurient, sadistic, impious men with such power often yielded to temptation. At its worst, slavery became a Negro purgatory, with slaveowners, slave drivers, and overseers twisting bravery into bestiality in orgies of lashings, beatings, and humiliations. Certainly these were exceptions to a general rule of humane and careful treatment, but exceptions which carried the violent strain.

The strain may be glimpsed in other ways. As John Hope Franklin shows in *The Militant South*, the section devoted much time to martial matters. Military schools, militia units, elite guard companies flourished below Mason and Dixon's line. Southern men claimed special prowess in the field, boasted their outdoors stamina, their custom to the saddle, their skill with guns—all requisites to the frontier and the code of chivalry in the South.

Wars have always fascinated young men of the region, and history has tolled the numbers of those killed, maimed, and blooded in battles for the nation. Southerners fought gallantly (an especially Southern word) at King's Mountain in the Revolution, at New Orleans in 1812, at Buena Vista, Monterey, Chapultepec in Mexico; and a close look will show the large part played by the South in leading the country into these conflicts. Once in the field, Southerners have proved formidable soldiers indeed—often undisciplined, finicky about their rights, suspicious of superiors, but infantry tireless and terrible. Martial pride persists in the Southland.

Politics persist, too, and as politicos Southerners have also shown the violent strain. Presumably the slave system gave planters sufficient free time to dabble in government and public affairs; hence they monopolized local offices and dominated party councils. Most Southerners were Democrats (with an occasional stray for sake of appearances), and most took their politics straight. Rural isolation, broken only by infrequent gatherings at county seats or forks of the creek, prescribed a system of personal politicking which suited the situation and the people. Southerners liked nothing better than a rip-roaring stump speaker who fulminated against his rivals with rolling periods and searing invective. A strong, undiluted rhetorical style gave a man character—especially if he aimed it at the character of others.

No other section of the country boasted such relentless zealots for the stump, the smoke-filled room, the ballot box. Southerners were uninhibited political animals—and to some extent still are.

Even as they cherished political fundamentalism, so, too, they cherished religious fundamentalism. God counted in Dixie. He counted in various ways, of course, according to persuasion, but in the Old South religion had a large part in daily life. People in the frontier areas, remote from eastern decorum, believed in a personal God, sought His favor, prayed with fervor and conviction. Religion came stronger to Southerners, doubtless because most of them lacked the sophistication of brethren in the North's Burnt-over District. Preachers, be they Methodist, Presbyterian, or Baptist (Episcopalians and Catholics were less demonstrative), rode their camp meetings, their circuits, or their pulpits fervidly and carried the Word with bombast sufficient to match the glibbest politician. Hell loomed real and awful every Sunday; brimstone billowed and burned; salvation came only with purging and penitence—and those who backslid or wandered from the path were branded by the lash of biblical oratory. Not all denominations, of course, pursued fundamentalist masochism, but even among sedate congregations in the South religion had stronger flavor than elsewhere. It still does.

This strain of violence, present in so many facets of the Southerner, might never have amounted to more than a dangerous crotchet had not a focus, a direction, been given it. Direction, purpose, if you will, came largely from the fact that the South developed along almost Hegelian lines. By this I mean that its character, its mores, its reactions, its violence, evolved in response to external (and sometimes internal) challenges. As things worked out, the South could never quite achieve a synthesis, for it usually failed to meet a challenge with the proper response. It attempted always to react, but in so doing, it often overreacted.

Since Southern action and reaction is my main thesis, let me elaborate a little. Some thirty-five years ago, in 1928, the famed Southern historian Ulrich B. Phillips published a significant article entitled "The Central Theme of Southern History," in which he argued that the one element in the South which made the land and people different was the resolve that Dixie "shall be and remain a white man's country." White supremacy forever, that was the battle cry which unified and stratified the section. Historians, and less turgid pundits, have agreed, but reluctantly. Recently, in fact, the Central Theme theory has come under heavy fire. The most perceptive analysis of reasons for the unpopularity of Phillips' idea is offered, I think, by Professor David Potter in his essay "The Enigma of the South" (*Yale Review*, LI [October, 1961], 142–51). Potter suggests that scholars shun the Phillips theme, not because he was wrong in what he said, but because of his "lack of moral indignation" in saying it. Acceptance of white supremacy as the immutable fact of the South is more than liberal students can tolerate. Potter accepts Phillips' conclusion, but adds an ingredient which provides a fresh interpretation of Southern life: while white supremacy does characterize part of the section, the element which distinguishes it from the rest of the country is the persistence of a folk culture. This "culture of the Folk," "full of inequality and wrong" as it was, nonetheless offers an alternative to the modern industrial leviathan and hence may be the reason for Dixie's haunting appeal.

Let me say that I agree that the South was, is, and probably will be, different from the rest of the country. I do not think that difference is necessarily evil. But I do suggest that response to challenge is a theme in Southern experience which is perhaps more constant than others. It is a theme compatible with both Phillips' and Potter's views. It focuses the deep currents of extremism in Southern blood, it explains the political, social, military, even economic behavior, and—to me, at least—it comprehends the South.

For my purposes, let me call this pattern of reaction to challenge the offensive-defense mechanism. I like this term, not only because I am a student of military history, but also because it is Jefferson Davis' own and hence has the best possible imprimatur!

To begin: It seems to me that the first clear-cut use of the Southern offensive-defense mechanism occurred in 1798 and found expression in the Virginia and Kentucky Resolutions. True, the South itself sustained no attacks in 1798, but Virginia and Kentucky expressed a lurking fear of federal encroachment on the Constitution which might lead to later oppression. Most important to the future of the South was the reaffirmation by Kentucky in 1799 of its objection to federal infringement and its assertion of nullification as a legitimate weapon against the "general government." Implicit in all these resolutions was the principle of state review of the Constitution and of federal legislation. This principle, worked finally into the doctrine of interposition, still beguiles the South.

For a time in the early nineteenth century Southern extremism took a firm nationalistic path. Such leaders as Clay and Calhoun labored to strengthen and unify the United States—even to the extent of preaching a jingoistic crusade against England in 1812. Gradually history appeared to work against the South's equal place in the Union, despite the luster of the Virginia dynasty. As far as the South could see, two ugly stains spread slowly across the image of the nation: industrialism and abolition. In the early years of the nineteenth century industrialism and its parasitic bureaucracy caused the greatest concern, but with the Missouri Compromise abolitionism came to a lingering, ominous prominence. These dual threats—unbridled capitalism spreading industry and federalism inexorably across the country; fanatical abolitionists striving to destroy the South's economic and social order—these threats demanded counterattack.

Initially the offensive-defense seemed moderate enough. Southern leaders worked for the Missouri Compromise, but for a highly sectional reason: they sought a chance to expand the South. Expansion figured prominently in Southern plans, since additional Southern states were essential to keeping a balance between the North and South in the Senate. If the agrarian system could expand westward below the line 36° 30', the perilous balance might be maintained and Northern nationalist and abolitionist legislation blocked. If the balance slipped, agrarian democracy was doomed along with slavery.

Clearly, though, the tide of Western civilization ran hard against Dixie. Try as it might, the South simply could not keep pace with Northern economic and political expansion. Cotton's kingdom looked prosperous enough at a casual glance, and the growing monopoly of world markets reinforced the illusion. Shrewd businessmen, though, and practiced judges of Southern economics, urged diversification and argued that agriculture could hardly stand alone. The South found itself caught in a trap of history—long addiction to staple production tied the planter to a factorage lien system and this, in turn, made diversification virtually impossible. Circumstances pushed the whole section steadily toward an almost mystical cotton idolatry.

Cotton proved a jealous idol. Grown in increasing abundance, it demanded expanding markets, consequently Southerners relied heavily on European trade. This made them especially uneasy about the effects on the price level of the federal tariff policy. The tariff question has all but disappeared from textbooks, but before the Civil War it ranked as one of the biggest snags in the fabric of union. After several incidents the controversy boiled over in 1832, following the passage of the ill-famed "tariff of abominations" and its highly protective successor. Southern reaction set in with deadly ferocity and centered in South Carolina (a special study ought sometime be made of why South Carolina blood runs so hot). The upshot of the trouble was nullification, nullification according to John C. Calhoun, with genuflection toward the Virginia and Kentucky Resolutions. South Carolina nullified the tariff law; President Andrew Jackson stood firm behind Congress' Force Bill and called the South's bluff. Although Henry Clay managed a compromise tariff which saved everyone's face, the lesson of 1832 could hardly be missed: nullification failed as a counterpoise to creeping federalism. That left only one final, ultimate weapon—secession. Before that last resort, however, many hoped that differences might be reconciled within the framework of the Constitution.

Southerners had long paraded their passion for the Constitution, and certain it is that they became the most legalistic of Americans. This led them to develop an elaborate constitutional argument as a kind of intermediate line of defense; strict constructionist dogma might make secession unnecessary.

It might have worked, save for a new issue arising in the 1840's, an issue beyond the scope of law—this issue was whether or not a slave-owner could take slaves into federal territories. Southerners saw no problem, of course, since private property could be taken anywhere in the country and enjoy protection of the laws. To the extent that they saw things, the Southerners were right. Their conception of the situation overlooked the fact, however, that many Northerners wanted to restrict slavery's spread. So the real issue came down to freedom versus slavery, free soil versus slavocracy. The whole touchy business was aggravated by the activities of New England emigrant aid societies, which poured money and settlers into Kansas and Nebraska in the 1850's. Again the offensive-defense: Southern groups rushed in a counterwave of emigrants to balance the scales. Skirmishing between both sides erupted into full-scale battles, and the bloody war in Kansas ran luridly across the nation's headlines throughout the decade.

Sadly for the South, the Kansas counterthrust proved too weak to restrict free soil. The appeal of free soil seemed irresistible. Even the spectacular court victory proclaimed in the Dred Scott decision of 1857 could not dim the portent of free soil's relentless spread.

Compromise, tried by both protagonists, narrowly averted a breach in 1850. The keystone of Henry Clay's compromise was a new Fugitive Slave Act; on its strict enforcement depended Southern acceptance of the entire package. But almost immediately various states north of Mason and Dixon's line began a campaign to nullify the act—they adopted the Personal Liberty Laws which gave freedom to all within their borders.

Such laws, of course, abrogated Clay's compromise, but the South stayed its violence for a time and sought protection under the Constitution. But there was almost no Northern co-operation and hence no protection under the law. This ultimate failure came at a tender time, for it showed clearly how hollow was the Dred Scott decision and pointed up the moral strength of the North's new Republican party.

Denied the Constitution, badgered by ceaseless abolitionist propaganda, the South wrapped itself in a burgeoning nationalism, and, reinforced by its conviction of slavery's "positive good," fell back on its last resort: secession.

Few responsible Southerners seriously advocated separation; most regarded it as a dangerous expedient to be avoided at virtually all costs. But the costs had finally mounted too high; the time had come at last to take the offensive against Yankee thraldom, to withdraw from a country without justice.

In the case of the Civil War the South took the offensive by seceding, the North reacted by resisting disunion, and the South then had to react to a war of unprecedented anger. Time would show the war as much more than a brothers' conflict, would make it a cleavage in life for the South. Beyond battles and dying and heroics, it became a kind of ultimate confrontation of the North, of civilization, of time itself. To this mysteriously fundamental struggle the South committed every man, every sinew; its tatterdemalion gray ranks never had enough men, food, guns, bullets, shoes, or medicine, but they held back history for four years.

Everything went with the war—energy, hope, blood, treasure. Sated with death and privation, Southern violence lay dormant through the early years of Reconstruction; dormant, but not dead. And it may well be that the greatest tragedy of Reconstruction is that it revitalized the violent strain through the real and fancied excesses in the "late rebel states." Instances of Yankee oppression and brutality brought on the old offensive-defense mechanism, that conditioned response which even the Civil War could not kill.

The initial Southern reaction aimed more at keeping a distinct place in the nation rather than at suppressing the black man. But the efforts of Radical leaders to put the "bottom rail on top" in Dixie, to deny whites any part in government while elevating the Negro to a status for which he was mentally and emotionally unprepared, produced resentment. Tragically, the Negro became the symbol of Southern degradation, the "cause of it all." Reaction focused on him, as dread bands of "ghosts" ranged the Southern countryside, first terrifying, then burning, flogging, scourging. Violence mounted as the Klansmen rode. Before this savage current ebbed again, misery and terror spanned the old Confederacy.

Oddly enough, Klan terrorism marks one of the few times the Southern offensive-defense mechanism won a victory. Radical Reconstruction doubtless faded for many reasons, but Southerners could argue from tangible evidence that their defiance brought salvation. So the violent strain fed on success.

After 1877 and the final "redemption" of the South, white supremacy did, indeed, become the hallmark of the section—that and a passion for the Yankee dollar. Violence could rest for a time since white rule was easily maintained by an occasional burning cross and the specter of the Klan.

The offensive-defense took a slightly different form through the 1880's and 1890's. Efforts centered on keeping conservative Democrats in power, on chilling supporters of radical farm and labor movements, on building a politically and socially solid South. Southern politicians found racist extremism a useful weapon in these campaigns. The time-worn catechism of "a white man's country" proved as persuasive as the tattered "Bloody Shirt."

Such wholehearted concentration on political control resulted in a kind of Southern isolationism which allowed the section to lapse into economic decay. Behind the cotton and racist curtains, procrustean leaders sought a split-level prosperity—one which would fatten the rich and starve the poor. They boasted the virtues of balanced budgets (achieved through such economies as truncated public school systems) and no public debts (achieved in some cases through repudiation), while living on Yankee capital induced to the South with promises of cheap land and labor. Forgotten in their stagnating enclave, Southern Bourbons built a shabby record of irresponsibility—and I say this despite some recent efforts to erect their perfidy into principle.

Isolation can breed conformity. It did in the South. And conformity, in a way, fitted into the pattern of offensive-defense. When next invoked, around the turn of the century, the mechanism focused on elements of unrest in the South itself. Populism and other radical isms posed threats to the status quo and had to be suppressed. Suppression was accomplished first by skilful brandishing of white supremacy and later, when unions loomed seriously, by tarring some of the labor movements with a Bolshevik brush.

Neglected and almost forgotten by the rest of the country, the South had few outlets for its violence for some years. But there had to be outlets—they were demanded by Southern nature. Fortunately some of the violence could be expended in legitimate ways. In 1898, for example, war with Spain offered a chance for another Southern crusade, and the whole section burned with martial ardor. And so it did during World War I, when Southern prowess at arms won added fame in the heroics of the dauntless Dixie Division.

Following World War I, at a time when the violent strain surely was sated with blood, the South continued along its poverty-ridden course. In the midst of the Great Depression the section ranked as the most depressed part of a depressed country. At first glance it seems miraculous that so little extremism occurred in the South in the 1930's, but it ceases to be surprising when the long history of penury is remembered. What violence there was during the depression had a familiar look. Textile workers, driven by unbearable privation, went on strike in some Southern mills. And wherever there was a strike, there was almost always violence. Irate fellow Southerners, traditionally dedicated to laissez faire, rioted in support of mill owners. Anyone who upset the time-honored order of things was un-Southern!

Negro workers always got the worst of the trouble, especially so during the depression. Lowest paid, they were the first to be fired. In the labor troubles of the early thirties they received the brunt of the violence. This was hardly new; the Klan had shaped the pattern of Negro persecution fifty years earlier, and the South followed it with increasing dedication. Even in the days of splendid isolation, the Negro knew no "salutary neglect." Shocking statistics on lynchings can be offered to show savagery bubbling to Dixie's placid surface in the half-century following Reconstruction. Diseases of all kinds, social, economic, political, found remedy in a good lynching, and resort to the hanging tree became a kind of Southern tribal rite. Some thought that spilling a little colored blood now and then might be a good thing for the South. Obviously it was the worst possible thing, and there were many people, increasingly many, who said so and worked to disband the necktie parties. But lynchings were symptoms, symptoms of latent uncertainty, hostility, and, most of all, fear. I think they represent a distinct facet of the offensive-defense mechanism, one that could be glimpsed in the earlier Klan activities and the threats of violence. They served notice on the Negro that he would remain inferior and on his Northern encouragers that the South would not be made over in Yankee image, would not lose its identity to onrushing bureaucracy.

To some extent the problem of Negro participation in Southern life had been assuaged by the famous *Plessy* vs. *Ferguson* decision in 1896.

Separate but equal public facilities created an illusion of equality and fixed the condition of second-class citizenship on the Negro. Jim Crow practice spread until Negroes moved automatically to the rear of anything, and a crippling subservience marred the manhood of their race.

It is true that tranquillity at length prevailed south of Mason and Dixon's line. The depression must take the credit for much of it, the Northern "hands-off" for some, and a true affection between black and white for the rest. Affection between the races is hard for present-day liberals to swallow. Herbert Aptheker, a modern historian, sees class warfare as constant between blacks and whites, finds incipient Negro revolts behind each headline, and looks toward a Marxist millennium to save the situation. The Progressive School of American historians, currently ascendant, sees only evil in slavery and segregation and doubts any shred of the myth about whites and blacks loving one another. Some did and some still do. May they increase!

Current tensions certainly started with the case of *Brown* vs. *Board of Education of Topeka* in May, 1954. This historic, long-overdue decision sought to redeem an unfulfilled promise of the Civil War. As C. Vann Woodward has perceptively said, the North had three war aims: first, to save the Union; second, to free the slave; third, to honor the pledge of equality proclaimed in the Declaration of Independence. The third war aim had not been achieved, but the promise had never lapsed.

On that fateful day in 1954, many Southerners believe, the tortuous progress in race relations (and they can point to some remarkable achievements during the last thirty years) stopped. The Supreme Court decision burst on the South as another external threat, almost as a neo-abolitionist attack. The long struggle was not over; the North still pursued its course toward complete, absolute domination.

Instantly the South reacted with the offensive-defense. The caption of the mechanism had always been: "We want to be left alone; you people up North don't understand our situation because you don't have Negroes in large numbers." But by 1954 things had changed, and the statement had no shred of truth to it. Negroes, segregation, and racial tensions were common in Northern cities, and relations between whites and blacks were often worse than in the South. So this new Yankee assault must be aimed not at uplifting the Negro but at destroying the identity of the South. What was it about the South the Yankee envied enough to hate?

Whatever the North's objective, the South needed a new battle cry to rally its defense. When it came, it had an ageless appeal, but also a viciousness missing before: "No integration, no mongrelization, no social degradation." The proud purity of the Anglo-Saxon was at stake now; school integration would obviously lead to social mixing; that, to miscegenation.

Direct action against the Court's decision built up slowly, with moderate voices raised in caution. The Klan was dead, or at least moribund, for which decent opinion in the South gave thanks, but the odious White Citizens Councils arose to lead the new offensive. I have seen something of these councils in action and can attest that in Louisiana, at least, they had little following at first. The venerable Southern tradition of *noblesse oblige*, often mistaken for arrogance, came to the fore, and there was a real chance that the decision would be honored in peace.

Extremism, in the long run, could not be denied. Demagoguery is a phase of it, and the Citizens Councils' demagogues rose to rant once again about the white man's country, the old order, the evils of Yankee aggression. By 1956 a significant shift toward the wilder strain had set in.

That summer I taught at Louisiana State University, situated in the state capital at Baton Rouge. A large number of Negro students enrolled in the graduate school, registration passed without incident, and the semester progressed. Negroes shared the dormitories, dining halls, and all graduate classes. I had an integrated class on Reconstruction and I have never had a more enlightening or encouraging time.

In the summer of 1957, I returned to the university and felt a subtle change of atmosphere. During the past year the legislature had spawned a senator of the violent segregationist stripe. Up from obscurity on the coattails of race-baiting, he co-operated at every chance with the Citizens Councils' fanatics. Governor Earl Long, not a race-baiter himself, could neither halt the activities of the councils nor silence the loud anti-Negro minority in the legislature. Consequently, a sickening, albeit interesting, campaign of intimidation began, aimed at Louisiana State University's Negro students. Some in my class suffered; one told me she had received a letter threatening her unless she dropped out of the university. There were other instances of veiled but unmistakable intimidation and at least one outburst of violence.

Numbers of Negroes dropped out of the university, of course, but an encouraging number stayed. At the end of the summer, the white curtain folded tighter over the campus as Louisiana committed itself to total resistance. The real tragedy in this story is that when Negroes first appeared in the university, white students made almost no protest—both races got along. Extremism caused the trouble, particularly extremism with a Little Rock tinge.

Segregation made a strong comeback after the Little Rock school crisis, largely because Little Rock was branded as another example of federal invasion, a direct attempt to suppress Southern individualism.

Although Governor Faubus lost his immediate fight, his example of brief defiance did lasting damage to the pattern of peaceful coexistence which, I think, had been forming. Bravery at the racial barricades became fashionable, a game of Rebel roulette which enabled demagogues to wave the Confederate flag in defense of things about the South which Lee or Davis or Stonewall Jackson would scarcely recognize and certainly loathe. There is a straight line of continuity between Little Rock, Prince Edward County, Virginia, New Orleans, and Oxford, Mississippi. In each of these episodes resentment grew until, in the last ones, violence again broke the surface.

In these recent outrages, however, it may be that the traditional pattern of offensive-defense is wearing a bit thin. More and more voices of moderation can be heard in the South; nothing is more encouraging, for it shows a significant fading of intellectual conformity. Without solid support, segregationist extremists are doomed to be defeated by their fellow Southerners, both white and black.

One of the most important things about the current situation is that Negroes are taking a large hand in the desegregation fight. Whether whites like it or not, the black man has begun to count in Dixie. Ignored for decades, tucked violently in his niche ("place" is the word), the Negro suffered without redress. Some whites feared that proper leadership could wake the black giant and bring problems aplenty, but there had to be something more than leadership.

First the long-standing pattern of Negro docility had to be altered. The Booker T. Washington–Black Sambo heritage had to go before Negroes could become true Southerners.

Courage and shining hope came to Negroes with the Supreme Court decision—and hope was desperately necessary to a race blighted by denial of its rights and dignities. Hope came too late for the older Negroes, broken into subservience, but younger generations, college trained, aware of democracy, caught a glimpse of equality, a glimpse of the promise lingering unfulfilled from the Civil War. This vision, and the hope it sustained, produced leaders and also touched the current of Southern violence in the black man. These new men inherited the Southern character, despite their skin, and once they discovered their manhood, they reacted against pressure with startling strength.

Sit-ins, stand-ins, silent strikes, appear to be forms of passive resistance, but considering the years of black docility they are fairly activist weapons. Disciplined moderation characterizes most instances of Negro offensive-defense, but here and there violence breaks the Stoicism—the recent unfortunate riot in the District of Columbia stadium being a case in point.

Negro violence, the result of unparalleled provocation, may be a type of "good violence." But wise leadership will be needed in the immediate future to restrain this old Southern trait, channel it, focus it.

Equal wisdom will be demanded of white leaders, who face the formidable task of reprogramming the mechanism of offensive-defense, even of sublimating it.

The best chance, I think, for full alliance of the races, for the survival of Southern identity, lies in this very mechanism—strange as it may sound. If all Southerners, black and white, come to recognize rabid racism as the worst threat facing the South, counteraction may set in and reason prevail.

I am by no means certain that prevail it will. Unfortunately, I fear that, before that happy day, much more violence will wrack the Southland. For Dixie is suffering the terrible agony of outside irritation and internal spasm. There is the possibility that a tradition as old as the section itself may enforce a reaction of moderation—the tradition of honor and responsibility represented by General Lee and, more recently, by South Carolina's Clemson College. Responsibility and concern for fellow men is the key to curbing the violent strain.

Southerners cannot change their spots or alter their chemistry. Land, climate, and blood will make them in future as hot-tempered and quick to resentment as ever. They will continue to rely on the offensive-defense mechanism, and it will probably cause as much trouble as it has in the past. But it is important to remember that the mechanism is triggered by aggravated provocation. Once this is realized, the Southern extremist makes sense. We may not be able to sympathize with him, but we can understand.

T. HARRY WILLIAMS

Trends in Southern Politics

T<small>HE POLITICIAN</small> has always been a man of moment in the South. He still is, even in an age when in more sophisticated sections other heroes —social engineers, industrial managers, and entertainers—have shouldered their way to the front of the stage once monopolized by the practitioners of government. In the states below Mason and Dixon's line politics is yet an art and a profession and a diversion, and the politician is honored among men. The practice of politics varies, of course, from state to state. To my knowledge, it is carried on with the most skill and style and most relentlessly and constantly in Louisiana. "Politics is to the conversation of Louisiana what horse racing is to England's," says A. J. Liebling. "In London, anybody from the Queen to a dustman will talk horses; in Louisiana, anyone from a society woman to a bellhop will talk politics. Louisiana politics is of an intensity and complexity that are matched, in my experience, only in the Republic of Lebanon." Like everybody else in the state, I am fascinated with politics and always ready to discuss it. My interest in it has been stimulated and, I believe, my understanding of it heightened by the course of five years of research on Huey Long, research that has led me into conversations with hundreds of politicians.

Once in American history "politician" was a good word. When people said of somebody, "He's a politician," they meant a man skilled or at least adept in the mechanisms of statecraft at the local, state, or national level. But eventually there came to be a subtle change in both the phrasing of the identification and the meaning behind it. Then—and if a date had to be set for the change it would be in the years right after 1865—people said, "He's just a politician," and the remark was definitely not complimentary. "He has a loose, shifty expression of face,"

T. HARRY WILLIAMS, Boyd Professor of History, Louisiana State University, a famed student of the Civil War and Reconstruction, is the author of *Lincoln and His Generals* and has just completed two volumes in the *Life* "History of the United States" series.

remarked E. L. Godkin in a typical evaluation, "and one which gives you the impression of a thorough politician." "I am not a politician," boasted Artemus Ward, "and my other habits are good." Mark Twain observed that he had got so he could look on a congressman without awe, even without embarrassment. Sophisticated people thought it was clever to say that a statesman was a dead politician.

The politician fell from his former estate for various reasons. Partly the fault was his. In the years between Appomattox and the turn of the new century many politicians in every area of government cast themselves as agents of powerful economic interests, either doing the bidding of these groups for material rewards or blackmailing the same groups for rewards with the threat of punitive legislation. At the same time the general level of ability among politicians dropped. As the businessman assumed a greater status in society, he became the new American folk hero, the man everyone aspired to be. Smart boys no longer thought the highest honor was to be President, senator, or governor. It was much more satisfying, and profitable, to be a Rockefeller or a Carnegie or a Morgan. The best brains went into business instead of into government. Gradually the politician became in the popular mind an ordinary fellow of no particular consequence or competence. He had, in the phrase of a later culture, a bad image.

The image grew with the years until it acquired the rigidity of a pattern. Helping to fix its mold were the students of politics, the writers of books and articles on its practice. They found little to praise and much to condemn in the conduct of politicians. Almost without exception these commentators were from the academic world, and they tended to impose the standards of their world upon another and very different area of activity. Their technique was unrealistic, and it has contributed to a wide misunderstanding of the function of the politician. In briefest essence, the academics have expected too much from the men of the hustings, the smoke-filled rooms, and the polls. The professors have thought that the politicians should act much like themselves: debating issues with calm, balance, and scholarly restraint; presenting plans of doctrine, detail, and logic; acting, in short, like sweet philosophers. That politicians do not conform to these standards is obvious—and shocking to the detached campus observers, who fail to realize that they are upholding impossible standards. The politicians could not exist if they acted like professors. The great political leaders particularly cannot fit their actions to any previously conceived set of rules or bind themselves to any abstract ideals. Such men—a Franklin D. Roosevelt, a Lincoln, a Napoleon, a Gandhi—have to follow their destiny. They make their own rules, and in moving to their goals they are quite likely to ignore the philosophers, or even to dispense with them altogether.

They may be, in Crane Brinton's aptly ominous words, "not philosopher-kings but philosopher-killers."

The academic analysts are responsible, along with an allied group—the moralists, the reformers, the "good people"—for popularizing another unrealistic concept of politics, the doctrine of what might be called the double standard. It demands that politicians be more honest than everybody else, that, in fact, they be completely and consistently honest, making no compromises and no concessions but standing always on eternal principles. To the reformers there is no mystery about what is the right course. It is only too apparent. Edwin O'Connor has one of his characters in *The Last Hurrah* say of reformers generally and of one in particular: "I mean they're so *serious* about being honest. And they're always so right. About everything, not just politics. There's this one little professor. . . . Jack says he's very bright. But he's just so serious and so *angry* about being right."

As anyone who takes even the most perfunctory interest in politics knows, the politicians are constantly making all kinds of deals and arrangements and concessions. This is disturbing to people who have been conditioned to believe that politics is a moral activity, and it is positively shocking when practiced by an officeholder who has won election as a reform or "good government" candidate. Then, particularly, the average voter is likely to conclude that he has been deceived, that all politicians are crooks, and that politics is an area beyond the concern of good men. The result is to induce a cynicism that turns interest away from government and may be highly dangerous to the democratic system itself.

We very much need to get all along the line, in the classroom and in the popular consciousness both North and South, a new and more realistic notion of the nature of politics. We must recognize that we must concede to the politicians what Henry Taylor asked the English to admit long ago: "A free judgment namely, though a most responsible one, in the weighing of specific against general evil." As distasteful as it may seem, we have to realize, for the sake of morality if for no other reason, that politicians have sometimes to do what we may think is evil so that they can do what we and they know is good.

Robert Penn Warren puts the case for the politician perfectly in *All the King's Men*, that book which whatever else it may be is a profound political treatise. Reformers want good things, says the Boss, Willie Stark, but they will not do the acts necessary to get them. They will not do even a little bad to accomplish great good. Of his attorney general Willie laments: "He resigned because he wanted to keep his little hands clean. He wanted the bricks but he just didn't know somebody has to paddle in the mud to make 'em." And of Stark's method Jack Burden observes: "The theory of historical costs, you might put it. All change costs something. You have to write off the costs against the gain. . . . Process as process is neither morally good nor morally bad. We may judge results but not process. The morally bad agent may perform the deed which is good."

This may seem too cynical a view to some, and to others it may seem to place too much freedom of choice in the hands of the politicians. But the disturbed may remember that no American leaders, not even the most powerful ones, operate without restraints. In the course of investigating the life of Huey Long, this writer has asked numerous Louisiana politicians, men who have held an office such as sheriff for twenty consecutive years, if Long was a dictator. The question is usually received with contempt, and nearly always the answer goes something like this: "What is a dictator? Somebody has to run the show, to make the thing work. They call me a dictator. They called the man I defeated one. And the man who beats me some day, they will call him a dictator." Their point, although not expressed with academic precision, is sound. No politician, no boss, no power-seeker can function in the American system indefinitely. He has to return to the electorate at regular intervals to continue to exist, and at any moment he may lose his identity.

If the politician is not a philosopher putting into effect eternal principles, what then is he? He is, and here we speak of what may be termed the ordinary or average politician, an adjuster and a broker of the many conflicting and competitive interests in a democratic society. His role is not to ram one set of interests through but to compromise with all of them so that everybody can live with the settlement. When the politician is considered in this framework, he immediately appears in a much more favorable stance—he is the man who makes democracy function. And, as T. V. Smith reminds us, when his vices are compared not with those of secluded individuals but with those of dictators almost beautiful things can be said of him. Says Smith: "People elsewhere get killed in the conflict of interests over which our politicians preside with vices short of crimes and with virtues not wholly unakin to magnanimity."

Most politicians are in politics because, although they will not always admit it, they love the game or the profession. It is in their blood. They may accept some rewards along the way, but the rewards are generally incidental. The politician labors at his trade every day in the year, and year after year. Because of him this funny thing that we call democracy works—and the rest of us have a large measure of freedom.

The typical politician adjusts current interests. But occasionally there arises a great politician who shakes the existing order. He seeks to change the context in which he has to operate, to sway people to move toward his own goal of good, to forge new combinations of power around new issues. Jacques Maritain calls him the prophet leader, the one who attempts to arouse men to a sense of something better than everyone's daily life. Eric Hoffer calls him the mass leader, the one who harnesses men's hunger and fear in the service of attaining the New Jerusalem. In the South we call him, sometimes with accuracy but more often because we are frightened of him, the demagogue. He is the great leader, and we always recognize him. "Without him the world would seem to us incomplete," writes Jacob Burckhardt. "He appears complete in every situation, but every situation at once seems to cramp him. He does not merely fill it. He may shatter it."

It is patently evident that Southern politicians have sometimes performed the functions required of the type and that at other times they have departed from them. They have often failed to adjust conflicting interests within the section, partly out of apathy or timidity, more frequently because popular opinion has seemed too monolithic to attempt to alter it. Nor have they been notably vigorous in seeking to reconcile Southern demands with national interests, but instead have stood forth as the champions of an unyielding sectional interest. The region has had its great leaders, the shakers of the existing order, the shatterers of old arrangements, but too often these men have started out with high ideals and then subsided into mere noisy breast-beaters.

For a long time, since the 1830's, as every historian knows, Southern politics has revolved too much around one issue, the issue of race. An inordinate amount of energy, time, and thought has been devoted to the defense of slavery first and then white supremacy. (Conversely, at times too much Northern effort has been devoted to attacking the thing the South was defending.) The result has been to invest Southern politics with an air of romance and unreality. The South has chosen to stake its destiny on one issue and to defend that issue with one strategy. It has glorified itself too much and looked inwardly on itself too little. It has acquired a garrison psychology. It has too often let its stand be determined by what the outside "enemy" was against. In the process the normal economic and group differences of a democratic society have been ignored and vitiated.

It can be argued that this inner unity of the South was, before 1860, the result of an identity of interests within the section. But even if the generalization is accepted as correct, which it is not completely, the same kind of statement cannot be made of the section after 1865. The New South was a land of diverse interests and occupations and peoples. And this modern South would witness expressions of social difference never seen in the Old South—the Populist protest, the farmer movements of the 1890's, and the Progressive surge after the turn of the century. There would be a great deal of noise in all these agitations, and there would be some legislation that looked to change. But the surprising thing is that after everything was over nothing much was very different. The Populists after a brave show disappeared from the scene; the agrarian reformers and the Progressives lingered on but were able to accomplish only mild revisions.

The failure of all these movements was epitomized in the career of Ben Tillman, who was influenced by the Populist crusade and who was a part of the agrarian and Progressive protest. Tillman denounced the rich in violent language, but despite his seemingly radical rhetoric he did practically nothing to uplift the life of the common farmers. "These men," says Phillips Russell, "he led within sight of the promised land and there he left them. But he could not have carried them further. As if realizing this they stood around uncertainly in the glare of the light for a moment, while a new stratum of politicians filtered through them and occupied the places of power. And then they went back to their farming."

The various reform movements failed for a combination of reasons. Their leaders might win office, but they were unable to destroy the power base of the opposition and hence could not perpetuate their control for any significant period. They aroused the emotions of the masses without satisfying the mass desire for a better life. Essentially the protesters failed because they could not overcome the tradition of the past and all the past represented—the Old South, the Lost Cause, and above all, the race question. The Populists tried to meet the race issue head on and were destroyed by it. The agrarians and the Progressives attempted to use the issue to distract attention from their own omissions and saw it run away with them. All of which is another way of saying that Southern politics was still romantic, still monolithic. Despite all the protests and the partial reforms, the salient fact about Southern life as the 1930's opened was poverty, grinding, abject poverty that afflicted most people of both races. In most Southern states the old ruling caste still held the reins of government. It was "government by goatee," by gentlemen in frock coats and wide hats. It was stuffy and stale, and it was almost oblivious to the cravings and needs of ordinary people.

That the Southern masses had not been satisfied by the superficial reform of the Progressives and that they were not content to remain indefinitely under the rule of the gentlemen was evidenced by the periodic appearance in different states of the leaders usually termed demagogues. Call them demagogues or mass leaders or prophet leaders, one fact about them stands out. Every one of them rode into office because he promised something that the masses wanted, and every one of them represented the hopes of the common people for a better life. The men dismissed as demagogues embodied a genuine popular revulsion against the stuffed shirts who ran the state governments, against the almost utter absence of any sense of responsibility on the part of the old conservatives.

The demagogues promised much. But they did not always deliver. Some of them found that they could not make delivery. They did not destroy the power base of the opposition and hence could accomplish only part of their program and were eventually hurled from power. Others did not seriously try to deliver and even sold out to the opposition. Still others, in frustration, took to beating the race issue and so continued the romanticism they had set out to dispel.

But one of the demagogues delivered—in a sensational, effective, and almost terrifying way. Huey P. Long became governor of Louisiana in 1928 and then, while still boss of the state, went on to the national Senate and to national fame and to a violent death in 1935. He was on the scene for only seven years, but in that short, explosive period he literally changed the face of Louisiana—and in the process he stirred the emotions of poor white people all over the South. Huey Long was different. He was a true mass leader, a shaker of the existing order, a leader who set up his own goals and inspired men to follow his road to new and hitherto undreamed-of Canaans.

Before Huey Long burst on the Louisiana scene, the state had the most extreme kind of government by goatee. The ruling caste had only the slightest notion of the transforming currents of thought sweeping the modern world and only the smallest sense of social responsibility to the masses. It was a state that had in effect stood still for a century. Long jerked it into the modern world practically overnight. Most of his opponents never understood why he overcame them so easily. Those who are alive today still do not understand. We were for honest government, they complain, and yet this fellow beat us. They do not realize that virtue alone was not enough in a period when thousands of people yearned for even elementary improvements in their way of living. "He destroyed our way of life," they will say over and over. He did not do quite that, but he did lift the life of the common people to a new and relatively decent level.

Long's program of good roads, expanded education, extended public health facilities, and enlarged social services was denounced as radical and socialistic and un-American. Actually, it was none of these. It was essentially moderate and pragmatic, and it could well have been furnished by the ruling caste years before—if they had had the sensitivity to grasp the need for it and had been willing to tax themselves to pay for it. What made his program seem so extreme was the way he put it through. Having no mind to be hamstrung by a lagging legislature, he resorted to the most ruthless methods to achieve his goals. Before he was through, he had erected a power structure unheard of in Southern politics and undreamed of any place else. He set out not just to eject the opposition from power but to destroy its base of power, its source of sustenance. A supreme power artist, he aimed to force the opposition into his organization on his terms and to control all branches of the state government, and he came close to succeeding.

It was a bold and imaginative scheme, but the lasting significance of Huey Long is not in the power machine he built. His great imperial structure was completely a personal creation, and it would not, as he well knew, survive him. His real importance rests on something more enduring. Of all the mass leaders he was the only one who forced an element of realism into Southern politics. He made people think about the problems of their own day. We do not live in the Old South, he said, or in the Civil War or in Reconstruction. We live now and we can solve our problems now. We should go forward instead of searching for a refuge in an imagined past. With essential accuracy Gerald Johnson, who did not admire Long's methods, could say that he was the first Southerner since Calhoun to extend the boundaries of political thought.

In Long's thinking the issues that mattered were those of economics and power. The issue of race that agitated so many politicians was to him an artificial and romantic question. He never seriously employed the race business to advance his own fortune or to damage an opponent. His concept of race relations was, for his time and environment, completely realistic. He cut the Negroes in on the lavish welfare program the state embarked on. He wanted to help poor people, and he knew that poor whites could not be aided without uplifting poor blacks. In 1935 he tried to explain his program to Roy Wilkins, the later Negro leader: "I'm for the poor man—all poor men. Black and white, they all gotta have a chance. They gotta have a home, a job and a decent education for their children. 'Every Man a King'—that's my slogan. That means every man, niggers along with the rest, but not especially for niggers." Wilkins was somewhat puzzled by the interview. "My guess is," he wrote, "that Huey is a hard, ambitious, practical politician. My further guess is that he wouldn't hesitate to throw Negroes to the wolves if it became necessary; neither would he hesitate to carry them along if the good they did him was greater than the harm."

Mr. Wilkins, who was as single-minded as some of the people on the opposite side, may be forgiven for missing the point. What Long was really saying was that he would carry the Negroes as far as he safely could at the moment. He would raise their economic and educational standards—because he could actually accomplish that. He would not attempt to extend the suffrage to them—because if he did he would fail and everything else that they had won would be lost. (But the suffrage grant would come under Huey's brother and heir, Earl Long.) In brief, Huey Long's strategy was to subordinate the race issue to what he considered a proper niche, to see that the Negroes made some advances, and to move both races along to higher economic levels. He destroyed in Louisiana the oneness that had always characterized Southern politics and put in its place an enduring pluralism and realism.

Today it seems clear that the South is moving into a more realistic political mood. Southerners who, more than other Americans, will have to endure the effect of wrenching changes in race relations, are coming to realize that they can be conservative on the race question without being romantic, without erecting that question into the only issue that matters. Perhaps more of them would be this way if people on the other side would recognize that the race problem, while it has to be solved, is not the only one that should absorb attention.

The present South needs certain qualities in its politicians, and if it expects to get them it will have to exhibit the same qualities in its people. What the South needs above all else is home-grown dissenters. We need to formulate our own social criticism without regard to what may be said in the North. We need to get rid of the garrison psychology that has too long affected the section. It is not necessary to assume a stance of defense against every censure from beyond the borders. The South could well do with less uninformed criticism from the outside. But it absolutely demands more informed criticism from the inside.

WALTER PRESCOTT WEBB

The South's Future Prospect

Just what I, primarily a western historian, am doing discussing the South needs some explaining. In this explaining I shall be rather personal as I tell of my relation to the South, and my deep interest in its future.

Though I was born in Texas and have lived in Texas all my life, my parents grew up near Aberdeen, Mississippi, during and after Reconstruction. They left Mississippi about 1885, at a time when young people had little chance to escape from the poverty which had been imposed on them by the Civil War and its aftermath. They brought their poverty to Texas with them, along with a lot of bitter stories, and I grew up on both. Though we gradually escaped the poverty, I never

WALTER PRESCOTT WEBB, late Professor of History, University of Texas, was one of the best known of American historians. A student of the West, he gained renown for *The Great Plains*, *The Texas Rangers*, and *The Great Frontier*. For several years he had been especially interested in the glittering future of the South. He had been working to stimulate Southerners to forget the past and seize the present. His paper was prepared shortly before his tragic death in an automobile crash on March 8, 1963. His paper was read by JOE B. FRANTZ, Professor of History, University of Texas. Professor Frantz prefaced the paper with the following remarks:

"I am here under false colors today—as a pinch hitter for the late Walter Prescott Webb. To pinch-hit for Dr. Webb is presumptuous; there is no such item as an adequate substitute. Not that Webb was a dynamic speaker or teacher. Indeed, he appeared to be a bit awkward and hesitant in everything except his written prose. But if he were awkward, it was the awkwardness that displayed more of forcefulness backed with immense reserves than almost any other quality.

"Webb came through. He convinced. Though he disliked those abstractions that have been mentioned intermittently here, you could say that his effectiveness represented a triumph for bluntness, for honesty of design, for simplicity in approach, and for power of purpose.

"Although he was multifaceted, one of his more profound facets was that of a promoter—of the Big Bend, of a consciousness among Texans that water is even more a precious resource than petroleum—a promoter of ideas, and of various unsuccessful liberal politicians.

"One of the ideas that had particularly possessed him for the past decade was that the South belongs in the driver's seat of Horizons Unlimited—that it is the great underexploited area of the nation, that it has let certain myths and protracted backward glances obscure its sense of forward direction—that it can well represent the galvanic force of the next several generations in the United States—and that only the South can now defeat the South."

escaped the stories. Their influence was such as to make me turn away from Southern history to the less tragic and more rambunctious story of the American West.

In 1937 I published a small volume entitled *Divided We Stand*, and in the preparation of this volume I backed into the South. In preparing that book I hit upon a simple device of dividing the nation into its three great natural regions, the North, the South, and the West. Then I measured the wealth of these three regions to find that while the South and West had about 85 per cent of the natural resources, the North owned about 80 per cent of the wealth and income. Though I knew the South was poor, I did not realize that it was so desperately poor as it was in the 1930's. Though I have not proved it, I think that I hit the South at its very nadir, at the lowest point economically relative to other sections that it had held since 1875. I do not mean that it had less wealth in 1930 than it had had in 1875, but that it had a lower percentage of the national wealth than during the earlier period. Though the South had 29 per cent of the national area and 27 per cent of the population, it had less than 5 per cent of the great corporations, less than 10 per cent of the wholesale firms, less than 4 per cent of the seventy-five leading life insurance companies, less than 3 per cent of the annual income from those companies, less than $11 out of each $100 in demand deposits, less than $6 out of each $100 of time deposits, and it paid less than $5 out of each $100 paid in income taxes. The same study showed that the South produced more than 45 per cent of the oil, nearly 40 per cent of the coal, more than 46 per cent of the lumber, and nearly 37 per cent of the sixty-four leading crops. I hardly need remind my readers which of the three sections, with 21 per cent of the area and nearly 58 per cent of the population, had 90 per cent of the large corporations, nearly 85 per cent of the wholesale distributors, 95 per cent of the large life insurance companies, nearly $80 out of each $100 in demand deposits, and more than $82 out of each $100 in time deposits. Nor do I need to remind you that this same section paid $84 out of each $100 in income tax; this area produced less than 5 per cent of the oil, less than 10 per cent of the lumber, and a little more than 36 per cent of the crops.

Our aim is not to upbraid the North for its overwhelming dominance of the economy of the nation at that time. No good would come of that. We may be permitted to point out as a fact, and to emphasize it, that the picture has changed in the last thirty years. It is the change, and the prospect of further change, with which we are concerned.

The plight of the South in the 1930's was such that it attracted national attention. There had been set up in Washington the National Emergency Council, for in the 1930's there were many emergencies. Lowell Mellett, Director of this Emergency Council, sent out a call to thirteen of the Southern states asking that representative citizens be sent to Washington to consider the Southern emergency.

The President of the United States addressed a letter to these men in which he dramatized the plight of their region.

It is my conviction [he said] that the South presents right now the Nation's No. 1 economic problem—the Nation's problem, not merely the South's. For we have an economic unbalance in the Nation as a whole, due to this very condition of the South.

It is an unbalance that can and must be righted, for the sake of the South and of the Nation.

When future historians, freed from the emotions of current politics, set out to find the pivot on which the South turned from its miserable past to its better present and far better future, they are likely to select this report as that pivot. Its value was that it diagnosed the case with a candor often lacking in diagnosis. The head doctor then told the nation that the malignancy of chronic poverty had to be treated for the sake of the region and for the sake of the nation. How can a nation be well when more than one-fourth of it is desperately ill?

The story of the South from the 1930's to the present has been a cheering story, and I now come back to my part in it. In *Divided We Stand*, I dramatized the unbalance mentioned by the President, dramatized it with stark figures from the most reliable sources, and I sought to explain the condition of the South through history. As the years passed, people constantly asked: "Do you not think that the condition of the South has improved since you made that study?" I had to say "yes" to this question because as I traveled over the land I saw signs everywhere that conditions were better than they had been. I saw fat cattle on green meadows, better farms and crops, and fresh paint on houses. I saw Southerners wearing good clothes, registering in the best hotels, carrying themselves with confidence into banks and business houses and coming out with what they went in for. They walked a little taller, and they found something in their pockets besides their empty hands.

But when I said "yes" to this recurring question, I was giving an opinion. I *thought* conditions had improved, but I did not know that they had, or to what extent. Then I determined to make a study of the situation as of the 1950 Census. I would measure the wealth as of 1930 and as of 1950 and see what had really happened to the South in twenty years. If what I found in the first study was depressing, what I found in the second was exciting. In every category of wealth examined, the South had made much relative progress, and in some cases its progress had been spectacular.

Let me give three examples. Of each $100 in demand deposits in 1930, the North had $78, the South $11, and the West $11. Twenty years later, in 1950, the North's share of that $100 had dropped from $78 to $60; the South's share had almost doubled, from $11 to $20; and the West's share had increased from $11 to $20. In that same period the individual's income had increased in each section. The Northern individual's income had increased 119 per cent; the Westerner's had increased 148 per cent; but the Southerner's had increased 223 per cent. In 1930 the South paid in individual income tax less than $5 out of each $100, but in 1950 the South paid three times as much, approximately $16 out of each $100.

Now I could answer the question, "Have conditions in the South improved?" in a bold affirmative. Not only have they improved, but at a greater rate than in any other section. It is my opinion that later censuses will reveal that the improvement has continued and accelerated, and that it is destined to continue unless we Southerners do something foolish.

By the time I had finished this second study, I had become reasonably familiar with the South and highly curious about its prospects. I did not believe, and I do not believe, that its progress is due to political action, though I would contend that political action in the 1930's did contribute to Southern progress. Anyway, I began to look at the South intimately, as I would look at a piece of real estate that I was figuring on buying. "What are its potentials?" I asked. "What are its natural advantages?" "Is it the sort of real estate that an investor would buy?"

As I held this condensed South in my hand, as I figuratively walked around it as I would a piece of land I could buy, these are some of the things I saw:

1. The South is the only region in the United States that fronts the sea on two sides. From Virginia to Key West, it looks east to Europe across the Atlantic; from Key West to Brownsville, it looks south to Latin America. The South's shore line along the Atlantic is 1,099 miles; along the Gulf it is 1,659 miles. It has a total shore line of 2,758 miles. It has nearly four times the shore line of the North, more than twice that of the Pacific coast, and nearly 600 miles more seacoast than the North and the West combined.[1] If there is a potential fortune in the sea, then the South has the easiest access to more than half of it.

[1] Shore line of the three sections:

		Miles
The North......................		789
The South		
Atlantic................	1,099	
Gulf..................	1,659	2,758
Pacific.........................		1,293
Total........................		4,840

2. It has one-third of the good farm land of the nation, and this land is now being made better by the year.

3. It has two-thirds of all the land with forty inches of rainfall or more, an asset too great to be measured.

4. It has a long growing season which gives it an advantage in the production of food and fiber, of livestock and feed. Because of these things, the South is the richest region in renewable resources. It was once a great natural forest. It is again becoming a great forest.

5. It has in the interior the greatest supply of fresh water in the nation, if we exclude the Great Lakes.

6. In minerals it produces 45 per cent of the oil, most of the sulphur, and it has enormous deposits of coal and iron which have hardly been touched. It is the region richest in natural resources.

Now I asked myself this question, I would like to ask it of every Southerner: Would you consider the purchase of a piece of real estate that had all these natural advantages, all this real and potential wealth? In short, would you buy the South as an investment? I think the time has come for us to start doing so.

As yet I have not touched on the industrial potential which is more immediately exciting than the natural resources on which the industrial potential is founded. I want to point out a silent revolution in technology which almost inevitably makes the industrial future of the South not only bright but brilliant. It is an industrial axiom that manufacturing is not based on a single resource but on a combination of resources. For example, such a combination of resources was found in Pennsylvania and West Virginia, consisting of coke and coal, iron ore, and limestone —all essential to the iron and steel industry. This trilogy ushered in the age of steel and did much to give the North its early dominance of the economy.

As yet little noticed is the fact that the South today has such a trilogy of resources which have combined to produce the petrochemical industry. This trilogy is oil and gas, sulphur, and fresh water. The South produces 45 per cent of the oil, a greater proportion of the gas, practically all the sulphur, and it has an unlimited supply of fresh water. I would not contend that the petrochemical industry will be as important to the economy as steel has been; I will say that its future is too great to be imagined at this time and that circumstances have conspired to make the South the center of its production.

At this point I want to tell you something about the South that I have never been able to tell to my own satisfaction. I have never been able to tell this story as clearly or as vividly as I see it. If I were a mystic, I would attribute the change in the South's situation to fate; if I were a scientist, I would say it is due to technology; and if I were a minister, I would say that the Lord himself, after permitting the people to suffer much, has finally come over on the side of the South.

I have a friend in Austin named Deacon Jones, a colored man of considerable wealth and deep religious feeling. He is a caterer, and he caters to white people who want to have picnics and beer busts on their ranches. I once made an appointment with Deacon to go out to the country, and on the way I asked him how he happened to get into catering. And this is his story:

Well [he said], I used to have a dray, and I hauled things for people. And then I got to stealing. I didn't exactly steal myself, for I am religious, but I got to hauling things for some men who was stealing hams and bacon and flour and sugar from a big wholesale house. They paid me double for hauling, and I done pretty well. But my conscience got to hurting me, for you see I am religious. I couldn't sleep at night, and I got to dreaming that the law was after me. And every time I saw the law I was scared. Finally, I quit and the men got awfully mad at me. Well, I couldn't get anything to do and me and my wife we almost starved to death. You see, the Lord He was testing me to see if I meant it, but I held out and finally things got better. You see, Mr. Webb, if you do right, and keep on doing it, the Lord will finally come over on your side.

I would not undertake to distribute credit for what has happened in and to the South among such three powerful claimants as fate, technology, and the Lord. As a historian who must have three reasons for any change, I am willing to accept all three, and I welcome all three to the side of the South.

We can see the transformation that has occurred by viewing the South as it was in the last century and as it is today. In the nineteenth century it was a tragic figure with many afflictions. Today it stands stripped of most of these old handicaps, sound and well on the threshold of a new era. Let us look at the obstacles that have fallen, one by one.

1. It used to be said, for example, that the South could not industrialize because it lacked fuel. Then came oil, of which the South has about 50 per cent of the nation's supply.

2. It used to be said that the South was handicapped by its hot and humid climate. Then came air conditioning, which is now almost universal.

3. It used to be said that the South could not grow beef cattle because there was not enough grass and too many ticks and flies. Then came the bulldozers to clear the land for grass and improved insecticides to kill the flies and ticks. The South is today rivaling the West in the production of fine cattle.

4. It used to be said that the South's soil was depleted. Then came scientific agriculture, soil-building practices, and the chemical production of fertilizers to repair the destruction.

5. It used to be said that the South could not compete with the Middle West in the production of pork and bacon and hams because it lacked corn. Then came milo maize which is now grown in the thousands of tons, and it is just as good pig feed as corn. The Southwest, where the maize is grown, can divide the hog market with Iowa.

6. Prior to the Civil War the South's network of rivers was a great economic asset because the rivers were used as transport routes for commerce. Then the railroads came and took away the importance of the rivers. But now modern industry requires enormous quantities of fresh water, and of this the South has the greatest unused supply. Big industry is covering the water front and moving inland along the river channels. The West cannot rival the South in heavy industry because of its lack of water. The North has water but it is already saturated with industry. Industry is coming South because there is really no other place for it to go.

7. It used to be said that the South could not develop its own re- sources because it lacked capital, and that used to be true. Now capital centers are developing in the great cities of the South, and it is no longer necessary to go North for capital in moderate amounts.

All of these things I saw, many of them for the first time, as I held the South in my hand and looked at it and asked: What of its future? How can such a land, so rich and so appealing, lie fallow?

Then it occurred to me that what is needed is a program for the South that will speed its development, a program so designed that the Southern people will share in the prosperity that is sweeping the land. I want the Southerner to see that the Lord has finally come over on his side. I want him to understand that

> There is a tide in the affairs of men,
> Which, taken at the flood, leads on to fortune,

and I want him to see that this tide is running now in all the bays and inlets, up the rivers, into the harbors, through the burgeoning cities, and over the green fields that were once eroded and sterile. And, I thought, if Southern people see this they will take hope, which they were nearly out of for a very long time. It is not easy to stir the Southerner's hope. He has been so accustomed to seeing the South play third fiddle that he has a hard time imagining it in the leading role. It shocks him somewhat to be told that the next century may well belong to the South.

The reason I want the Southerner to see all this is that I want him to become a gambler. I want him to risk his money on the future of his own land. I want him to spend his capital with the confidence of the speculator who feels sure of the return. I want him to act as the good poker-player acts when the cards are falling right and he is getting his rushes. I want him to get rich just for the novelty of it, and then I want him to use his wealth for the further development of his own land, for the improvement of his own farms, for the eradication of the last vestiges of disease, and above all for the better education of his children. And I want him to get so busy doing these things that he will forget the past with all its tragedy and turn his eyes to the future, which is all he has left. I want him to make a land that his talented sons and daughters will remain in rather than leave. Whereas in the past the South has imported capital and exported its talent, I want it to become an exporter of capital and an importer of talent.

Feeling as I have come to feel about the South, I suppose I have turned myself into a propagandist. I began to tell my tale to various audiences who would listen, and to give them the evidence I had gathered as to the future prospect. I was invited by a great Northern university to a conference on the industrialization of the South, and I found there a large number of Southern industrialists. I was a little curious why this Northern university would exhibit such interest, and then I heard a rumor that disturbed me. The great university was launching an endowment drive for $30,000,000, and this conference was used to attract attention of Southern businessmen and industrialists who might prove useful. The rumor may have been no more than a rumor, but I do know that my suggestion of an all-South conference to be held at Atlanta or New Orleans met with no response. I also know that in the final discussion session, the whole pack took off on the racial question, which consumed the entire time.

In telling my tale I ran into all the reasons why the South cannot do what I envision.

The first reason is that the South *does not want to change*. And there is some truth in this contention. Up in Virginia I told my tale to audiences in five colleges and universities. At one small college I spoke in the morning, and I thought I had told an inspiring story. At the luncheon that followed, I expected, or hoped, to hear some discussion of the future and bright prospect of the South. It was never mentioned. The entire conversation, ramrodded by a local minister, was about where George Washington slept, who built this house when, and who was kin to whom. But at the University of Virginia I fared much better, finding there a young man who may well become a real leader in the Southern renaissance.

In *Editor and Publisher* (October 31, 1953) devoted to "Today's South," I found a story by Hodding Carter illustrating my point, namely, that the South does not want to change.

When the Scout Troop met, three scouts showed up who had not done a good deed that day. The scoutmaster wanted a perfect record, and so he sent the boys onto the street to do their good deed. They were back in about thirty minutes.

"What did you do?" he asked the first boy.

"I helped an old lady across the street."

"Well, that's fine. And what did you do?" he asked the second boy.

"I helped *him* help the old lady cross the street."

Though the scoutmaster was doubtful about this good deed, he accepted.

"What did you do?" he asked the third boy.

"I helped them help the old lady cross the street," he said.

"Now boys, you can't do this to me," said the scoutmaster. "This is ridiculous that three of you would want credit for helping one old lady cross the street. That's a job for just one boy."

"No, sir. It took all of us to do it."

"Why?"

"Because, sir, she didn't want to cross."

We cannot deny that many people do not want the South to cross the street and that it is going to take several boys to get her to do it.

The second reason given for the probable failure of the Southerner to grasp the economic opportunity before him is that he is so concerned with the racial issue that he has no time for anything else. We all recognize the force of this argument, and we must admit that, unfortunately, it has some validity. This is the issue that has plagued the South since 1820, and even if the Southerner himself would be willing to bypass it, there are those who will not permit him to do so. But I think we should seek to bypass the racial issue and get on with the main business. If I had a corps of a thousand men and women who would go out on a crusade to tell the tale of the future South, I would impose upon them but one rule. And that rule is that under no circumstances should they permit themselves to be drawn into more than a casual discussion of the racial issue. I am told by those who know the deep South better than I that this is an impossibility, but it is a worthy ideal, and we can try.

Toward the racial question, I think we should take the course Lincoln took toward Brigham Young and the Mormons during the Civil War. Lincoln's advisers came to him, asking:

"Mr. President, what are you going to do about Brigham Young and those Mormons in Utah? What goes on out there is a disgrace. What are you going to do about it?"

"I'm going to do about Brigham Young," said Mr. Lincoln, "just what I used to do when I was plowing a field where one of those hickory trees had fallen. That tree was too heavy to move and too green to burn, *and so I just plowed around it,* and for the present that is what I am going to do about Brigham Young."

The racial issue is too heavy to move; it is too green to burn; and so the best we can do for the present is to plow around it and cultivate the rest of the field.

The third and, in some ways, the most disturbing argument made against the prospect of a great future for the South came from an unexpected source, from a distinguished educator. I wrote an article entitled "The South's Call to Greatness: A Challenge to All Southerners," in which I set forth my view of the prospect. From this educator came a paper replying to my optimism. The title of this paper was: "The South Will Surely Fail."

The reason the author gave for the South's probable failure was that it is far behind in education, that its attitude toward education is antiquated, that it does not understand the importance of pure research or support it, that it has no really first-class graduate schools, that it exports its best students, and that it staffs its colleges and universities with second- or third-rate men from the big universities. He selected one of the top universities which had celebrated its seventy-fifth anniversary with much fanfare and boasting of progress. Yes, he said, that university has made progress, but what we lose sight of is that all universities are making progress, and that progress is accelerating at a tremendous rate. This particular university now ranks sixteenth in the nation among its class. If it continues its same rate of progress, by 1975 it will rank twenty-fourth. It is dropping further and further behind.

This man had his figures, where figures were relevant, and I could not give him any argument. I did say that the South's lag in education is due to its economic lag, and that if the South will improve its economic situation, it will have funds for education and for research. I am not giving the name of this educator because I do not wish to create prejudice against him for telling the truth as he found it. As a matter of fact, his observations on higher education in the South are supported by a recent seminar study of elementary and secondary education. Thirteen students made a study of thirteen states, each student studying a different state. When they put their findings together, they were unanimous in the opinion that the South's greatest deficiency today is in the field of education and in educational support.

These three obstacles to the program of Southern progress—not wanting to cross the street, overconcern with the racial issue, and a deficiency in education from the first grade to the research laboratory—constitute a burden that the South must pick up and carry. The time has come for it to cross the street, when it should reduce the racial issue to the category of minor problems, when it should tackle the educational problem with new insight and great determination.

In spite of the burden the South has carried, it has already made great progress. I could overwhelm you with statistics and specific examples to prove it. But instead of giving statistics I'll tell you two stories. The first story, told by Henry W. Grady, describes the South in 1889. Grady said:

I attended a funeral once in Pickens county in my state (Georgia). This funeral was peculiarly sad. It was a poor fellow like most Southerners. . . . They buried him in the midst of a marble quarry: they cut through solid marble to make his grave; and yet a little tombstone they put above him was from Vermont. They buried him in the heart of a pine forest, and yet the pine coffin was imported from Cincinnati. They buried him within touch of an iron mine, and yet the nails in his coffin and the iron in the shovel that dug his grave were imported from Pittsburg. They buried him by the side of the best sheep-grazing country on the earth, and yet the wool in the coffin bands and the coffin bands themselves were brought from the North. The South didn't furnish a thing on earth for that funeral but the corpse and the hole in the ground.

The second story was told exactly seventy years later when the South furnished more for its funerals than the corpse and the hole in the ground. It was told by Arthur W. Wiebel in 1959. Mr. Wiebel had related the progress of the South as he had seen it from Alabama, and had noted with regret that this marvelous story was not getting the headlines. In concluding, he said:

And that . . . is the story [of the South] that has not made the headlines. If events of a more emotional flavor push it from the front page today, you may be sure that historians of a later time will give it the recognition it deserves. Whatever dissensions and disharmonies may beset us . . . the course toward the future is set; and nothing can check our progress toward a better day. The busy humming of our factories and the ringing of our cash registers are going to overwhelm the clamor of hysterical debate.

Since I have been telling a personal story, I might as well conclude by saying what I would like to see happen. I would like to see the members of this audience help three boys help the lady across the street. I would like to see a South-wide conference called in some centrally located Southern city. To this conference three groups should be invited:

1. There should be a few educators from the colleges and universities, but not too many. They could supply statistical information.

2. The second, and in many ways the most important, contingent would consist of Southern businessmen who understand the economic forces at work in the region. They would bring practical experience. The public will listen to them when it will not listen to the professors.

3. The third group would consist of one or two of the best students from each Southern university and from some of the colleges. The purpose would be to inform them of the prospects ahead, make them leaders

in the diffusion of this knowledge among their contemporaries, who will soon be in charge of our affairs.

The idea would be that these three good scouts—professors, businessmen, and students—would return home to spread the good news and the information that supports it. In preparation, I would like to see each graduate school in the South set up a seminar on this problem we have been considering.

In about one year from this first conference, a second one would be called in which an effort would be made to have all Southern governors present. The purpose would be to get the governors to unite in presenting the case to their respective legislatures and thus engage their interest in the movement.

Finally, I would like to see a spectacular documentary film prepared on the South today, showing the progress already made and the prospect ahead. And I would like to see the Southern Newspaper Publishers Association keep an eye on this program and back it for the mutual benefit of us all. While it sounds heroic to say, "I'll live and die in Dixie," there is nothing new or original about it. We have been doing both now for a long time. Since I hate poverty and love life, I'd rather be able to say, "Let's live—and prosper—in Dixie."

HUGH B. PATTERSON, JR.

A Look Forward

THE PRESIDENT of the Southern Newspaper Publishers Association is given the responsibility for arranging that organization's annual convention program. When I was given that opportunity for the year 1960, on the eve of the centennial of the Civil War, I thought it appropriate that we consider the future of the South and the role that Southern newspapers could play in helping shape that future.

Having been deeply impressed by a number of articles Dr. Walter Prescott Webb had written on the subject, I sought his advice and assistance in arranging that program, and he consented to give the keynote address. Through that experience I had the good fortune to come to know one of the great scholars of the South's history, and one of our region's most knowledgeable and vigorous advocates.

It is fitting that this symposium should include a posthumous paper by Dr. Webb, and that his work should be further memorialized through our continuing efforts to bring about the renaissance of the South which he foresaw, and to which he devoted so much of his thought and energy.

Though he always had time for thought and discussion of the South's future, he was impatient with the kind of academic meeting where, in his words, "they meet, talk, and talk, and talk, and go home and do nothing." And in corresponding with him only recently on this question, he wrote me on February 22, 1963, "I shall certainly do all I can to help promote the renaissance of the South."

Dr. Webb and the distinguished group of scholars represented in this volume have brought us a wealth of information and new insight into the South, and into the prospects for her future.

This is a new language of the South; a language of potential riches rather than poverty, a language of challenge rather than resignation, a

HUGH B. PATTERSON, JR., Publisher, *Arkansas Gazette*, Little Rock, is an active force in newspaper publishing. He has an abiding interest in Webb's plan for the future of the South and is working to stimulate responses from all parts of the section.

language of true pride in region unfettered and unclouded by a bitter and difficult past.

They are saying, in part, that with her natural resources, the South will develop in spite of herself; but that the time is here for Southern leaders to move up the timetable and to gain for her people, now, the blessings of a richer and more abundant life.

They are saying we have all the necessary elements, including modest but improving capital resources, for changing our area from the raw-materials economy, which has returned a meager yield from the earth and the labors of our people, to an economy based on modern industry, industry home grown and home owned to the greatest practical degree, where the retained profits of workers and owners alike can combine to produce higher standards of life and culture for all our people.

But they are also pointing to our deficiencies, and to those things that are continuing impediments to our growth and development.

And so what I would like to discuss, primarily, is the creation of a widespread but healthy atmosphere of dissatisfaction throughout the South with things as they are; an atmosphere that will breed healthy changes in the attitudes and aspirations of our people.

Certainly the South has made impressive progress since the great depression of the thirties, when the President of the United States characterized the region as the nation's No. 1 economic problem and pointed out that this was the nation's problem, not merely the South's. But the progress has been spotty, and we still find ourselves, as a region, lagging far behind the nation in our income and in our ability to provide the levels of public and private services needed for our people. And in considering the pace of progress in the South, we cannot but in honesty admit that an accelerated and encouraging rate of industrial and economic development in the last decade was retarded and, in places in the South, brought to a complete halt by the turmoil over the integration of public schools and public facilities.

As our experience of recent years at Little Rock bore testimony, outside industry steers clear of turmoil and strife. Expansion of existing industry is stifled, and potentially profitable ventures are depressed and made subject to exploitation by shrewd opportunists frequently operating in the realm of inside political preference and sanction.

Good new industry seeks localities with stable state and local governments, consistent and equitable tax laws and administration, uniform and effective law enforcement. Good industry wants good schools, good housing, good medical services, good cultural and recreational facilities. Repeated studies have shown the marked parallel between the levels of average educational achievement of an area and of the area's average income. Each of these requisites for economic growth calls for substan-

tial additional public and private investment, and it can be fairly observed that our region is already taxing itself for public services at a
percentage rate of income in excess of the national average.

This appears on its surface to be a difficult economic puzzle, and I for
one have felt that certain types of federal assistance could be justified as
an economic investment in raising the South, permanently, to a position
of equity and parity with the rest of the country. But if the question is,
"Which comes first, the facilities or the industry?" we have only to
look to our sister state of North Carolina, perhaps the industrial pace-
setter of the South in relation to her natural resources, and remember
that her political leaders at the turn of the century placed the state's
highest priority on public education. And we can further recall from
recent events that Governor Terry Sanford, in the fall of 1960, won
election against vigorous opposition while committing his administration to the preservation and strengthening of public education in that
state and to the raising of educational standards to equal or surpass the
national average.

Though in our economy, needs must be thoughtfully weighed and
priorities carefully established for our public institutions and programs,
these forces for progress can be complementary and concurrent with
industrial growth and are finally dependent upon the character of our
political leadership.

Our schools of higher learning in the South have, separately, done
important research bearing on our economy. Through the workings of
the Southern Regional Education Board, there has been some important
exchange of information between our state-supported universities and
the elimination of some duplication of costly teaching facilities and staffs
through the interchange of students in various specialized fields. Our
different state, governmental, and private industrial development or-
ganizations have exchanged some ideas through their associations.

But I believe the time is now here for our business and financial
leaders, our scholars, researchers, and educators, in public and private
institutions, to all join forces in developing the full range of our natural
wealth and economic potential. Let's ask them to join forces, South-
wide, in research programs and studies, free of political domination or
distorting influences, to identify our economic opportunities and to
publicize them for the information, the inspiration, and the action of our
people. And let's ask them to determine, through objective research, the
impediments, real or fancied, which have stood in the way of our progress. In every case of raw-materials export, whether agricultural, min-
eral, or forest resource, let us know why those materials were not proc-
essed in the South. Let's question whether vested interests are preserv-
ing outmoded methods or patterns of operations, perhaps still profitable

for themselves, but failing to provide maximum economic returns to their locales. Let's educate ourselves against economic exploitation from without or within. Let's ask the leaders of our great Southern financial institutions to intensify their interest in the development of Southern resources and in the research programs to support this development.

And while we are creating this healthy atmosphere of discontent with things as they are, let's take a new close look at the administration of our public affairs and institutions. Let's ask our professional administrators to make the best possible use of public funds in the operation of our schools, our housing agencies, our health and welfare services, and our law enforcement agencies. In this time of great need and unique opportunity, can we not look to our community leaders to set aside pride or jealousy or petty selfishness in order to consolidate undersized school districts and administrative school units so that children may benefit from better school curriculums and facilities. Is it not now reasonable to question whether our counties, cities, and towns might in many instances merge or combine such services as public health; police and fire protection; street, road, and highway maintenance; or other services that duplicate administrative overhead and equipment? Hasn't the time finally come when we should seriously consider overhauling much of our system of state, county, and local governments made obsolete by modern travel and communications, to make them more efficient and responsive to present needs?

Above all else, the progress of the South demands continuing, fully responsible, political leadership. This character of leadership is needed at all levels of our government; but most of all, for the South, we must have responsibility in those we elect to our highest state offices and to the Congress. These are the most influential political positions, and it is in these positions that default in leadership is most telling for a state or for the region. Here, of course, I am speaking in part of the recent tragic events in the South, when some of our political leaders, called upon for the best within them, too often responded with their worst; and rather than use their high offices and great influence for maintaining reason and order, instead contributed to turmoil and strife.

It is in such political default, indeed it has been through the failure of political leaders to face the simple truth calmly, that the South has suffered its severest reverses. In an address to the Harvard Law School in 1915, Oliver Wendell Holmes said, in commenting on respect for law and order, "When the ignorant are taught to doubt, they do not know what they safely can believe."

And so I feel it is time for us to call upon those who would aspire to our public offices to give us true, positive, constructive, knowledgeable, responsible leadership, or otherwise to move aside for those who will.